scm centrebooks

T G A Baker

What is the New Testament?

SCM PRESS LTD

SBN 334 01766 9
First published 1969
by SCM Press Ltd
56 Bloomsbury Street London WC1

© *SCM Press Ltd 1969*

Printed in Great Britain by
Billing & Sons Limited
Guildford and London

Contents

Foreword

The aim of this little book is twofold: first to give an outline of an approach to the New Testament literature which is characteristic of modern biblical scholarship, and with which the reader may be comparatively unfamiliar; secondly to deal with some of the vital issues which such an approach raises for our understanding and evaluation of the Christian faith. The first interest is predominant in chapters 1–6, the second in chapters 7–10. The difficulty all along has been one of compression, and of knowing what to include and what to leave out. Rightly or wrongly I have decided not to include very much in the way of background material, nor have I dealt in any detail with the content of the teaching of Jesus, or of the theology of Paul. These subjects are dealt with more fully in some of the books listed for further reading on page 126. More serious has been the problem of doing justice to the complexities of NT studies, and the varieties of interpretation, without loss of clarity and direction. As I was re-reading the manuscript before publication, I was tempted to pepper the text with such qualifications as 'perhaps', 'probably', 'though some scholars take a different view', and the like. It seemed best, however, to avoid such inelegant and wearisome repetitions, even at the risk of incurring the charge of dogmatism or over-simplification, but instead to invite the reader to make a generous use of the pepper pot in providing his own qualifications where he senses the need of them.

However, a word should be said about one particular omission, and that concerns the nature of the link or links which bind the New Testament to the Old. In the companion volume to this book, *What about the Old Testament?*, John Bowden makes the point that it is quite impossible to ignore or reject the Old Testament without having to drop about half of the New Testament as well, for the roots of the latter lie very deep in the former. Time and again the New Testament picks up ideas and images of the Old, and reinterprets them in the light of future events. I have not developed this point explicitly, nor attempted to define the precise relationship between the two Testaments. This is partly because John Bowden's book and my own, though planned together, were written quite independently; and partly for reasons of compression and selection. I hope, however, that it will be clear to the reader that this link is implied throughout the whole of this book. For example, where in chapter 2 it is stated that the Christian community is the matrix out of which the whole NT springs, it should be remembered that all the first members of this community were themselves Jews, who drew their concepts of God and their outlook on human life and history from OT perspectives, and who indeed thought of themselves as being the newly constituted Israel of God, and therefore heirs to the OT promises; consequently they used many of the traditions and images drawn from the OT to interpret their own experience as Christians. Again, in the chapter on Paul it should be obvious that the theology of the apostle presupposes many OT ideas and perspectives, both on the positive and negative side, so that it cannot be understood at all except against this background. The comments on the Logos doctrine of the Fourth Gospel, contained in chapter 6, shows how deep are its roots in OT conceptions, however much it may also be indebted to other ideas derived from late Judaism and Hellenistic thought. As I say, the link between the two Testaments is everywhere presupposed, but no attempt has been made to define the nature of this link. In fact the whole problem of the extent to which the Old Testament should be understood in the light of the New is a very complicated one for Christian theology and biblical exposition, and is at present being hotly debated.[1] What

7

cannot possibly be denied is that the New Testament *must* be understood, in part at least, in the light of the Old.

No originality is claimed for the ideas expressed in this volume. Where I have been consciously aware of my indebtedness to other books and sources, I have acknowledged this in the text or in notes. There must be instances, however, where such indebtedness is no longer conscious on my part, so that here I must simply express my gratitude to those whose ideas and insights have informed and fertilized my own. Finally, I want to express my appreciation of many useful comments and suggestions made by the Reverend David Mealand, and of his kindness in reading the proofs; and also my gratitude to several generations of theological students, at Lincoln and Wells, for their long-suffering in listening to the lectures on which some of the material in this book is based.

Wells
September 1968

NOTE

1. See James Barr, *Old and New in Interpretation* (1966).

1 Introduction

The New Testament is such a familiar possession that we easily fail to realize how oddly ill-assorted are the books which comprise it. The volume is all bits and pieces. It begins promisingly enough with what appears at first blush to be a biography of its main character. But then follow two further accounts of his life, in which many of the episodes are simply repeated, though often with rather startling discrepancies. Then comes a fourth account, obviously about the same person, but with few real points of contact with the previous three. Then we have what looks like a history of the early Church, but which on closer inspection turns out to be, from a historical viewpoint, singularly unbalanced, and which appears to peter out inconclusively at the end. After this we have a collection of letters by various authors. Some appear to be genuine correspondence dealing with specific matters of concern, while others turn out to be more like sermons or theological treatises. Finally there comes a totally different kind of document, which appears to be describing, in highly coloured language, the future course of history and the end of the world. Certainly the figure of Jesus Christ dominates the entire literature, but in all other respects it is indeed curiously fragmentary and ill-assorted.

Yet we have no difficulty in regarding it as one book. Surely one reason for this must be that the writings it contains have become the sacred and inspired scripture of the Christian Church. They are put out under one cover, not because of their homogeneity, but because of the unique authority which has come to be attached to them. These are the documents to which the Church appeals as its title deeds. If somebody asks what Christianity is all about, he is likely to be told 'read the NT'. The evangelical Christian finds in his daily Bible reading his chief spiritual sustenance and way to God. The catholic Christian is accustomed to hearing certain parts of the NT said or sung in public worship, often surrounded by high ceremonial, the gospel book being carried in procession, amid lights and incense.

But does not the NT derive its unity from having Jesus Christ as its central concern? Only in a limited sense, for there are thousands of other such books, written during and after the first century, but not included in these pages. So it remains true that the NT presents itself to us as one book mainly because of its status as sacred scripture. Now the process whereby these writings, and these only, received such authority, was a long and complicated one, exceedingly tedious to relate. It is sufficient for our present purpose to say that the process probably began in the latter half of the first century with the collecting together of a number of Paul's letters. This may have resulted from the interest in the Apostle engendered by the publication of the book of Acts. It may have been done at the hands of the author of Ephesians, himself a devoted disciple of Paul, though not the apostle himself.[1] Then as the literature of the Church increased, it was natural that the main centres of Christianity (Rome, Antioch, Ephesus, etc.) should collect their own libraries, a process which was hastened by improved communications between these centres. Next arose the conception of an *authorized* collection, or 'canon' as it later came to be called, and hence the distinction between literature bearing the 'imprimatur' of the Church and that regarded as less reliable or positively misleading. This process was itself hastened by the action of one named Marcion, who in the interests of his heterodox brand of Christianity formed his own self-authorized collection, consisting of one gospel only (Luke) and an expurgated edition of the Pauline correspondence. The Church, therefore, was forced to make up its mind which books it should

10

authorize. So throughout the second century each church centre busied itself with producing such an authorized collection, the criteria being apostolic authorship (direct or mediate), orthodoxy, antiquity, and suitability for liturgical use. Naturally each local church's list differed somewhat from that of its neighbours, but by the end of the century the core of the canon had taken shape, consisting of the four gospels, Paul's epistles, Acts, and some other epistles. Argument continued about such books as Hebrews, II Peter and III John, Jude, James and Revelation. Moreover, some of the books not contained in our NT (e.g. the Shepherd of Hermas) were included in some lists. In the early fourth century the church historian Eusebius divided the writings into three groups – recognized, disputed and spurious; and for a long time there continued to be disagreement about the class labelled 'disputed'. But it is clear that by this time the NT canon as we know it was virtually fixed. In 367 Athanasius laid down as canonical the twenty-seven books contained in our NT, and formal sanction was given to this list at a synod in Carthage in 397. So by the year 400 the NT canon was complete and fixed.

From this time onwards, therefore, it became natural to think of the NT as a single book, the inspired and sacred scripture of the Church. Now it is not my intention to deny that the formation of such a sacred scripture was part of God's providential ordering of his Church – but more of that in the final chapter. What is difficult to deny, however, is that the collecting together of these books into one volume of sacred scripture has in fact led to a manner of interpreting them which has always to an extent distorted their meaning, and which, if persisted in, will make them increasingly meaningless, irrelevant and incredible as the years go by. It is tempting to label this approach 'fundamentalist'; but it is better to avoid such blanket expressions, for the approach in question is certainly not confined to those who might accept, or rightly be described by, this label. It lies behind many a pronouncement made by members of Church Assembly, when some delicate and intricate problem of

11

contemporary ethics is settled by reference to a NT text, isolated from its historical setting, and treated as a divine oracle valid for all occasions. The trouble with this approach, so influential in the past, is that it is radically non-historical. It treats all the statements of the NT as if they had been sent down from above, unrelated to their original setting in life, unaffected by the relativities of all human conceptualizing, standing in no need of reinterpretation in the light of changing circumstances. Moreover, all parts of the NT are treated as being on one level, so that a proposition in one book is 'harmonized' with a proposition in another book, regardless of the fact that they belong to very different life-situations and areas of discourse, with different sets of presuppositions and categories of thought behind them. The richness and variety of the NT witness is obscured. It is assumed that Christianity consists in one single doctrinal and ethical scheme, in a set of interlocking propositions; and all the NT affirmations are forced together into the pattern. They are treated atomistically, each one being gently or forcibly removed from its own frame of reference in order to fit into another overall pattern to which it does not belong. The individual authors are treated as if they wrote in splendid isolation from the problems, needs and uncertainties of the community of which they were members, the Holy Spirit guiding their pen so as to by-pass their own individuality and the developing life of the Church which provided their setting.

All this, of course, is exaggerated and over-simplified, and the subject will constantly recur. However, it is vital in a book of this kind to emphasize at an early stage the importance of seeing each of the NT books against its own historical background, and of getting the point that this background is in every case the continuing and developing life of the Church – its worship, sacraments, preaching, teaching – its mission to the world, and its evolving institutions. If we are to get under the skin of the various authors, we must for a time forget that the books form one single canon of scripture, and treat them all separately, each in relation to its own unique setting. It is also important to remember that the books themselves came into being through a long and complex process, and something must be known about this process if we are not to get them wrong. Not only was the collection of books into a canon the result of such a process, so also was the composition of most of the books individually. This will be seen to be particularly true of the gospels, but it also applies to the epistles, many of which are much more composite documents than at first sight appears.

It is therefore helpful to be constantly reminding ourselves that the NT books were not deliberately written as 'sacred scripture'. Most of the authors thought that the world was shortly coming to an end, and would have been immensely surprised to learn that their occasional and often hasty productions were to be preserved for generations, and to appear under cover of a volume with 'Holy Bible' on its title page. One may safely surmise that, had they been so aware, they would have been a good deal more careful and circumspect in what they wrote. Paul might well have tidied up some of his obscure passages, and toned down some of the ruder comments he makes about certain of his fellow Christians! In passing it may be noted how absurd it is to try to find precise meaning, or profound contemporary relevance, in any and every passage, or to suppose that the authors were any more clear-minded, precise or consistent than we often are ourselves – especially when we, like some of them, are writing in the heat of the moment. If, for example, Paul had been asked some years after he wrote it precisely what he meant by the obscure and elaborate allegory about Sarah and Hagar in Gal. 4.21–26, he might well have shaken his head sadly and admitted that, if once he knew, he certainly couldn't remember now! Yes, the NT is at every point a very *human* document. How otherwise could it possibly communicate the truth of him who was the Word made *flesh*?

Another of those obvious facts, so obvious that they are easily overlooked, is that the Church managed to get on quite well for at least two hundred years without a NT, and had to wait four hundred years before it knew exactly what was in it and what was not. Certainly it possessed all that knowledge and inspiration which the NT was formed in order to conserve. Nevertheless it carried on its mission, celebrated its sacraments, consolidated its common life, knew the power of the Spirit and the living presence of Christ, without benefit of its own sacred scripture. Of course, in so far as it concerned itself quite early on with producing a literature to preserve the initial witness to the words and work of the Son of God, it might be said to have been in process of forming a sacred scripture. Still, it was a very un-selfconscious process. What is clear is that Christianity was never a 'religion of a book', even if later it tended to become one, as had happened with the religion of Israel. It would not even be true to say that the canon of scripture was definitively closed in 397, or that the NT then became, *in toto* and in isolation, the sole or supreme authority in the Church. The Roman Church and the Eastern Churches have always given to living tradition a place of authority along-side that of the scriptures. Anglican divines have tended to appeal also to reason and the contemporary mind of the Church. The continental reformers were inclined to dis-tinguish between those books which best conveyed what they regarded as the heart of the gospel and those which did so more problematically. We remember that Luther described James as an epistle of straw, and said of it 'I cannot place it among the right canonical works', though he adds that there are some quite good things in it, and that he doesn't mind if other people choose to keep it in the canon. Calvin is more conservative, but even he admits that there is doubt about some books. At the present time a very lively debate is going on between Roman Catholic and Protestant theologians as to whether it is proper to allow a 'canon within the canon' (i.e. distinguish between the authority of some parts of the NT as against others), and if so by what criteria. It is not only Liberalism but classical Protestantism and official Catholicism which in some ways

14

sit remarkably lightly (though in rather different postures) to the NT *as such*, though both give ultimate authority to the truth which it enshrines. No, Christianity has never been simply the religion of a book, not even in those branches of the Church which emphasize most the authority of scripture.

This last statement, however, needs one qualification, because from the beginning the Church acknowledged the authority of an already existing body of sacred scriptures, namely the OT. This was because the Church regarded itself as the true successor of ancient Israel as the people of God, and therefore the inheritors of its scriptures. Indeed, these writings were constantly appealed to in support of its own claim that Jesus was the Christ, i.e. the one who should fulfil all the promises made by God to Israel of old. Though not a religion of a book, Christianity began its life under the authority of a body of scripture believed to be inspired of God, and to which it gave a distinctive interpretation. Yet there were a number of factors operating which modified the Christian attitude towards these books, so that they did not find so dominant a place as in later Judaism. In the first place, the early Christians believed that the Spirit was once again active amongst them, and spoke directly through their 'prophets'. Secondly, they acknowledged another authority alongside, and indeed superior to, that of the ancient scriptures, namely the words of Jesus as transmitted in the oral tradition. Thirdly, they could not forget that, in many of these sayings, their Lord had treated these scriptures with remarkable freedom, himself claiming to speak with a higher authority, and going so far sometimes as to correct some of the old commandments. Men who believed all this could hardly be enslaved to the letter of the ancient scriptures, however highly they respected them as being a real, though not final, revelation of the one true God. In fact the authors of the NT books are highly selective in their use of OT texts, ignoring many, and modifying others. The NT is deeply influenced by, but not dominated by, the OT, because not all the OT expectations were equally suitable to

15

interpret Jesus as the Christ. The use which the Church made of the ancient scriptures was never slavish or rigid, but rather selective and creative.

So when all due allowance has been made for the high belief which the first Christians entertained concerning the inspiration of the OT, and for the growth of its own scriptures, it remains true that the mainspring of the Church's life is not to be found either in the ancient scriptures nor in its own sacred writings, however greatly revered. Rather all these writings, together with the use of the older ones, are related at every point to the faith, mission, sacraments and common life of the Christian community. We are thus prepared to see the NT as the record or transcript of a developing community life, rather than as a uniform collection of static and entirely homogeneous propositions. We are prepared to see the various parts of it (Paul, early Acts, Mark, John, etc.) as the literary crystallization of successive stages in the life, thought, and worship of the early Church. The NT has to be seen always against the background of the community which gave it birth and brought it to maturity. So now it is time to try to establish the truth of this approach by taking a closer look at the way the books of the NT took shape. But first we must attempt to discover the ultimate source, or matrix, from which all the writings derive.

NOTE

1. See E. J. Goodspeed, *The Meaning of Ephesians* (1933).

2 Community, Event and Message

The obvious answer to give to anyone who asks about the source from which the NT springs is, quite simply, Jesus Christ. In more than one important sense this would be a true answer. If Jesus had never lived, there would have been no Church and no NT. Yet this answer, as sometimes stated, can be positively misleading. It is misleading when it is implied that we possess in the NT some account of the life of Jesus, prior to and independent of the interpretation of him given in the more obviously theological parts of it, and in the faith and worship of the early Church. It is just not possible to take a look at the 'objective facts' concerning him, and on that basis decide whether or not we may accept the interpretation and the faith, the first somehow proving or demonstrating the latter. The NT itself forbids such an enterprise. Indeed there are good grounds for supposing that *in general* Jesus lived the kind of life, and possessed the kind of character which are delineated in the gospels, as a later chapter will attempt to show. But the first Christians were not interested in recording with any exactitude or detail the events of his life or the elements in his personality, from a neutral standpoint. Rather, he held a place of supreme authority in their hearts because of what they believed God had *effected* through him, and of which they had *present* experience. That is why they called him 'the Christ' (in Hebrew 'Messiah'). The Christ, in their expectation, was the one through whom God would create a new order, or a new humanity. Through their life together in the Christian community they experienced its blessings so compellingly that they found it hard to believe that the old evil order

17

could possibly last much longer. God's promises, enshrined in the OT, were being fulfilled through all that Jesus had done and suffered. Hence the oft-repeated 'according to the scriptures'. For this reason the Jesus they present is at every point a highly interpreted Jesus, not least in the gospel accounts.

We may note at this juncture that when St Paul and others use the expression 'Jesus Christ', they mean something more than a particular individual in past history. It is rather a short-hand expression comprising at least three notions: (a) Jesus as a figure in history; (b) the community in which he is present as the living Lord, the source of a new humanity; and (c) an event, or series of events, centring in the cross and resurrection, through which God acted for the world's salvation. In other words, the events of the life of Jesus receive their significance in the light of that community-experience which they brought to birth, and thus in the light of God's purposes.

So we are faced with a 'No road' sign, if we try to discover the source of NT faith in some 'objective' knowledge of Jesus, independent of that interpretation of him which we find everywhere in the biblical record. So let us try another path, and see if we can find this source in the very *earliest* interpretation of Jesus that we can discover. Many scholars are of the opinion that we can indeed discover such a primitive interpretation of a definite and indeed stereotyped kind.[1] This has been called the 'kerygma', a Greek term meaning the message proclaimed by a herald. Its main components can be discovered by placing together (a) certain passages from Paul's epistles, in which he appears to be transmitting the authoritative tradition of the Church, and (b) passages from the sermons of the Apostles recorded in Acts, which are similar in content and vocabulary. Taken together these comprise a kind of primitive creed, which can be summarized thus: 1. In the coming of Jesus Christ the purposes of God revealed in the OT are fulfilled, and the 'new order' of Jewish expectation has been inaugurated. 2. Jesus was born of the seed of David. 3. He lived on

18

earth as a man, teaching with authority, doing good, and healing the sick. 4. He died for us according to the scriptures, to deliver us from the powers of this evil age. 5. He was buried, rose on the third day, and appeared to certain chosen witnesses. 6. He is exalted to God's right hand, as Son of God, and Lord of living and dead. 7. As such he is the head of a new Israel, a restored humanity, on which God has poured out his Spirit. 8. Within this community is offered the forgiveness of sins. 9. He will come again to judge the world and bring to full realization the new order already inaugurated.

Now it would be most unwise to be over-dogmatic about this reconstruction of the primitive kerygma. It may not have taken the same form everywhere; in fact there is reason to think that not all of its clauses are equally primitive. As so outlined, it may have been the outcome of a process of development, however rapid. Still, there is little reason to doubt that this outline summarizes fairly enough what very early Christian proclamation was like. It represents the general way in which Christian faith first clothed itself in propositional form, and may thus be held to be in the nature of a primitive statement of belief.

But it would be a mistake of the first magnitude to imagine that here, in isolation, we have reached the source or matrix of all the NT writings, still less the ground of its unity. In the first place, this early propositional pattern was temporary and soon displaced by others, as the Church came into contact with the gentile world where Jewish messianic expectations were relatively unknown, and not compelling; displaced also by the very distinctiveness and originality of Christian experience demanding fresh and more adequate expression. In the second place, no form of words or credal expression can ever do justice to that basic faith-experience which both precedes and transcends it. Faith is response, not to a proposition, but to a reality which encounters, moves, challenges and even compels; which is inseparable from commitment; and which is tested by being acted upon. The propositions which faith uses to express itself are always provisional, relative to the thought patterns of the day, never to be identified with the reality itself. Creeds are useful maps, but never to be confused with the territory itself. If anybody doubts this, let him read again the 'kerygma' outlined above, and ask if, on its own, it would ever convert a fly – even a first-century Palestinian fly – let alone one of the twentieth-century European variety.

What then was the reality which grasped the first Christian converts and turned their lives upside down? The question can be answered simply.[2] It consisted in the actual, concrete experience of belonging to an equally concrete and actual new community, in principle coterminous with humanity itself; a community with a highly distinctive style of life, in which were offered gifts and opportunities not to be found elsewhere. To be sure this community life was at every point grounded in and controlled by the 'event' of Jesus Christ (the things he did, said and suffered), in which it had its origin.[3] But the only knowledge we can have of this event, and the only thing which made it the kind of event it was, lies in the concrete reality of that community life which came into being around it. We must now consider, therefore, what kind of community there was; and we shall in this chapter confine ourselves mainly to our two earliest witnesses, Paul and early Acts. In both places we are presented with an overwhelming reality which, again in both places, is summarized by the word 'Spirit'.

The story of the coming of the Spirit at Pentecost, as told in Acts 2, is so evidently the end product of a long process of development in which reminiscence, symbol and legend are inextricably mingled, that it is quite impossible to recover with any certainty the occurrence which gave rise to it. Yet there is every reason to believe that the symbolism expresses very accurately the experience of the first Christians and the nature of the community in which it happened. The experience comprised the following elements:[4]   1. It was an encounter with a reality which grasped and overwhelmed them, having about it an element of surprise. Though they were waiting for something, what occurred far outstripped these expectations. 2. It served to dispel those threats to faith which the ignominious death of Jesus had engendered. It was closely associated with the significance of the resurrection, a point which comes out even more clearly in the fourth gospel, where the giving of the Spirit is made to coincide with the appearance of the Risen Lord on Easter Day. 3. It immediately created a community of love and mutual sharing. 4. It created a unity broad and deep enough to overcome all barriers of race, class and culture. 5. It engendered a strong sense of mission to the whole world. Those who were grasped by the grace of this experience felt the need to spread the news of it so that it might become universally available. It should be added that this creation of new community immediately resulted in gatherings for worship and sacramental rites: Baptism as the means of initiation, the Eucharist as the means of growth. Lastly, it cannot be too strongly emphasized that, though the experience of new life in the Spirit was 'subjective' in the sense that it was directly 'felt', it was in its essence an experience of something 'given', originating in a divine act, not of human contriving.

When we turn to the Epistles of Paul, we find the same insistence on the Spirit as in Acts. To be sure his use of the word differs in varying contexts, and there are notable differences between his ideas and those of the author of Acts. But his general meaning is similar to the outline just given. For him the Spirit is, not an idea, not a doctrine, but an experienced reality. For him the Spirit is identical with the distinctive life-principle of the Church (note in Rom. 8.2 he uses the phrases 'Spirit' and 'life in Christ Jesus' interchangeably). For him the Spirit is nothing other than the actual substance or dynamism of life in Christ Jesus, viz. the life of the Church, expressing itself most eminently in the fruits of love, joy, peace, patience, kindness, goodness, faithfulness, gentleness, self-control. For him the Spirit is essentially that quality which is constitutive of, and the most characteristic element in, the Christian community – the Spirit *is* this distinctive thing for which a distinctive name was required: *agape*. Finally, for Paul the Spirit 'comes', 'is poured out'. It is not in any way self-generated. The Spirit is quite simply God himself in his boundless self-giving love towards men, offering new possibilities of freedom and community.

So now perhaps we have come to the end of our quest. Perhaps we have discovered the source or matrix out of which the whole NT springs. It is the concrete reality of the Church, with its equally concrete and direct experience of the Spirit, expressing itself in worship, sacrament and mission and embracing every area of human concern. Well, yes, we have. But at this point we must immediately let in by the back door the two candidates we have shown out at the front. For this concrete experience of new community was from the beginning quite inseparable, *both* from the historic event of Jesus Christ, *and* from the 'kerygma' or doctrinal formulation in which it had to express and communicate itself. For the Spirit which the first Christians knew in their midst was inseparably related to the actual impact made by Jesus on those who knew and followed him, both before his death, and infinitely more compellingly after it, in the light of the resurrection faith. The Spirit was the means whereby this impact was perpetuated in the community. The Spirit which they knew in their midst was one with the Spirit which was remembered to have been present in Jesus. Through the Spirit the character of Jesus, and his relationship with his Father, was reproduced and represented. Thus the Spirit was none other than the Spirit of Christ, the means of his continuing impact and presence among his own. By their direct exposure to the person of Jesus, both before and after his death, the Apostles were constituted the community of the Spirit, enjoying a relationship with God and one another than which nothing greater or fuller could be conceived. That is why no claim could be too great to make about the person and work of Christ.

The NT is the written deposit of the many and various ways in which this Spirit-giving encounter was transmitted to others in the earliest days of the Church. It was thus a most vital part of the work of the Church to transmit this encounter, this 'disclosure situation' in such a way that it continued to be the carrier of the Spirit. The actual reality of the Church's life, which *is* the Spirit, was originated by the impact of the things concerning Jesus upon those who knew him, together with their meditations and reflections on what they continued to mean to them. After this, the life in the Spirit had to be nourished by the continued 'remembering' of Jesus, together with the continuing effort to find ways of expressing it, communicating it, and drawing implications from it. Thus although the essential meaning of the Christ event was the coming into being of the Christian Church, yet the life of the Church was always inseparable from the need to communicate the memory of Jesus, and to clothe its experience in the only way in which it could be clothed, that is in already existing ideas and images. Indeed, the matrix of the NT is the coming into being and continuing life of the Christian community. But this life included within itself *both* the memory of the event of Christ (of which event it may be said to have been a part) *and* the 'kerygma', or verbal proclamation. But we now know better than to claim either for the 'life of Jesus' or the earliest 'kerygma' some purely *independent* priority, so that we might first establish their validity, and on that basis go on to assess 'objectively' the developing experience of the Church, and so set rigid limits to its capacity for fresh development – whether in worship, mission, sacramental structure, doctrinal formulation and new areas of human concern. It is only through commitment to and participation in the on-going movement of the community's life that any man can know Jesus as Lord (in the fullest sense), or make head or tail of any 'kerygma', ancient or modern.

Summing up this part of the argument: the matrix out of which the NT springs is the coming into being, and developing life of the early Christian community, understood as the nucleus of a new humanity, and itself under the continuing impact of the originating event of Christ. The actual literature of the NT is concerned (*a*) to articulate the concrete faith-experience of the community in a great wealth of imagery; (b) to communicate it in terms of accepted ideas which made sense to people, the early 'kerygma' being the first and in some ways normative attempt; and (c) to draw out the implications for life, worship and mission.

If this analysis is fair, we might expect to find traces of a rich, living and growing tradition behind the first written documents. Jesus himself left nothing in writing. Nor did he leave behind, after the fashion of a conventional rabbi or sage, a corpus of teaching already pre-packaged by himself so as to be easily remembered in exact detail. The effort of a small minority of modern (Scandinavian) scholars[5] to argue such a case has won little acceptance, even if it contains a grain of truth. The only thing that Jesus left behind was a living fellowship, conscious of itself as the reconstituted people of God in the world. Since this community was concerned to transmit, not a body of timeless truths, but a message about what God had done through a human life, together with an invitation to respond to what God was continuing to do through his Spirit, it might again be expected that this work would be carried on through the living voice of its members, and in the setting of its assemblies for worship and sacraments. We might imagine the leaders of the community proclaiming to would-be converts the salient points of the Christian message, handing on reminiscences of the words and works of Jesus, together with their comments upon them, leading its corporate worship, celebrating its sacraments, instructing those preparing for baptism, giving pastoral and moral guidance to the faithful. We might further expect that some of this material would soon tend to develop into set forms and patterns. All this we might imagine. But it would be more than an *a priori* judgment. The documents themselves provide plenty of evidence of it. As we read them, we keep stumbling on set patterns of preaching, bits and pieces of formal catechetical instruction, embryo creeds, and fragments of liturgy – all of which must have taken shape long before the authors of the documents in which they appear put pen to paper.

Thus we have already noticed clear traces of stereotyped forms of proclamation or preaching in Acts and the Epistles of Paul. There are examples of creeds in the making, as in Phil. 2.5–11. Then we come across fragments of hymns, in Eph. 5.14, I Tim. 3.16, I Cor. 2.9, and many parts of Revelation. There are examples of prayers which had been used in actual practice long before they were committed to writing, notably the Lord's Prayer. There are examples of liturgical formulations which had doubtless taken shape before being written down, as in the highly stylized accounts of the Last Supper, both in Paul's letter to the Corinthians and in the gospel records. There are numerous examples of catachetical instruction and formal codes of conduct, as in Col. 3.18 to 4.1; Eph. 5.22 ff.; Titus 2.2 ff. – to say nothing of other early Christian writings not included in the NT. There are also lists of regulations for church government, especially in the Gospel of Matthew, and in the Pastoral Epistles. All these circulated in oral form long before they came to be written down.

But we have left until last the most extensive type of material which took shape before any of it came to be written, and this consists in episodes from the life of Jesus, together with his words and teaching. So now we are prepared for an approach to the written gospels which sees them, not as direct eye-witness accounts, but as the final stage of a long and complex process going on within the corporate life and worship and mission of the early Church.

NOTES

1. See C. H. Dodd, *The Apostolic Preaching and its Development* (1936); C. F. Evans, 'The Kerygma', *Journal of Theological Studies* VII (1956), pp. 25–41.

2. The argument developed in this chapter owes much to the thought of Professor John Knox, particularly as it is brought to focus in *The Church and the Reality of Christ* (1962).

3. When the word 'event' is used in these chapters, it is intended to signify the total reality of the things which Jesus did and suffered, including in some sense their impact upon his earliest followers, both before and after his death – it therefore includes all that may be meant by 'resurrection'.

4. See Paul Tillich, *Systematic Theology* III (1966), pp. 160–162.

5. H. Riesenfeld, *The Gospel Tradition and its Beginnings* (1957), and B. Gerhardsson, *Memory and Manuscript* (1961).

3 Behind the Gospels

Most Christians are aware that the Lord's Prayer is recorded in the gospels in two differing forms, but are prevented by over-familiarity from seeing the implications. Unless we take the view that Jesus taught two forms of the prayer, a view not likely to commend itself to anyone of intelligence and with no axe to grind, we are forced to the conclusions: (1) that the first Christians did not scruple to adapt and expand the prayer as they taught it and prayed it; (2) that this adaptation took at least two forms, presumably as it was handed on in different areas; (3) that no difficulty was felt about attributing to Jesus a prayer which as actually used was an adaptation of his precise words; (4) that the prayer as recorded in our gospels has a history behind it, and represents the final stage of a process within the Church's life. Think now of a well-known conundrum in gospel study. In Mark 10.18, Jesus is recorded as saying, 'Why do you call me good? No one is good but God alone.' But in Matt. 19.17 we read, 'Why do you *ask me about* what is good? One there is who is good.' Again, unless we take the desperate expedient of assuming that Jesus said both things in connection with an incident which happened in the same way twice, we must conclude that his words have been modified in Matthew's version, presumably because of doctrinal interests. Consider now the ways in which the story of the Feeding of the Multitude, as told in all four gospels, immediately calls to mind the Church's celebration of the Eucharist. Note the language about the orderly arrangement of the 'congregation', the taking of the elements, the breaking of the bread, the giving of thanks, the distribution, first to the disciples then to the people. The most likely conclusion is that the actual experience of eucharistic worship has strongly coloured the telling of the story, so that it tells us as much about this worship as it does about what precisely Jesus did with the loaves and fishes. The story has a history behind it, and is not a direct eye-witness account. Consider, lastly, the prominent place given in the gospels, especially Mark, to the solemn and detailed predictions which Jesus makes of his own passion and resurrection. Now there are strong reasons which historical criticism can bring for the view that these do not, as they stand, represent the precise words of Jesus. But an untutored, commonsense approach leads to a similar conclusion, since it is exceedingly hard to account for the complete unpreparedness of the disciples for the events as they happened, if they had been predicted so frequently, so solemnly, and in such detail. Here we seem to have a statement about what the Church had come to believe about Christ's destiny in the light of the Easter events, rather than a direct report of his actual words.

It is considerations such as these which put a question mark against what may fairly be called the popular impression about how the gospels were written. This is to the effect that the writers set about their task much as a modern biographer might do. Thus it might be supposed that one fine day Mark decided that it was high time that somebody attempted the first biography of Jesus, and thought he would have a try. So first he looked around for any letters, reports or other documents which might provide material. Finding a dearth of such material (for his subject had written nothing himself, and nobody appeared to have kept any written record), he then made contact with as many eye-witnesses of the events as he could find, and made copious notes of what they had to say, being careful to record it exactly. Finally he put it all together in chronological order, and produced a book which he might have called 'Jesus Christ – a biography by John Mark'. It is thus tacitly assumed that there is a direct connection between the events as they were witnessed and the first written reports of them. But the phenomena mentioned above suggest the possibility that in between there had occurred a process within the corporate life of the Church, a process of reflection, adaptation and assimilation. The gospels then appear as the product and embodiment of this process. It follows that they stand at some stages removed from the events they record. It follows also that they are best seen as the product of a community effort rather than as exclusively the work of private individuals.

However, it may be objected that the examples mentioned are just isolated instances, and do not of themselves justify such a departure from the popular view. So at this point it is necessary to introduce on to the scene the work of modern literary and historical criticism of the NT, since by the use of these methods it is possible to show that these are far more than isolated examples, and that the whole of the gospel material, not just a few parts of it, is the end product of a process of development within the community life and worship of the early Church. It may therefore be helpful to digress at this point, and attempt a thumbnail sketch of that literary and historical study which has produced this fresh understanding of the gospel narratives.

Beginning where we are, with the first three gospels in our hands, we ask first how they are related to each other as literary compositions. We are faced at once with what has come to be called the 'Synoptic Problem'. This is no new problem. It was just as apparent to the early Fathers as it is to ourselves that these gospels are strikingly similar, and yet just as strikingly diverge very often when recounting what is obviously the same incident. Augustine solved the problem by assuming that Matthew was written first, and that Mark copied and abbreviated it. This solution held the field until the advent of a more scientific method in the nineteenth century resulted in the propounding of a solution diametrically opposed to that of Augustine. The chief tool used in this method is a 'Synopsis', i.e. the text of the first three gospels arranged in parallel columns. When the texts are viewed in this way, it becomes abundantly clear that, where the accounts run parallel, it is Matthew who appears to abbreviate Mark, and not vice versa. But other important factors emerge. 1. Matthew contains the substance of 600 out of the 661 verses contained in Mark, while Luke has at least 350 of the Marcan verses. 2. Though Matthew and Luke often differ in detail from the Marcan account, they rarely agree with each other in doing so. If they did, it might suggest that they were copying from each other, or using a common source other than Mark; but such agreements are rare. 3. Wherever Matthew and Luke diverge from Mark, each inserts the non-Marcan material in quite different sequence and order from the other. 4. They both appear to improve the Marcan style, and to clarify his story.

It has therefore been concluded that Matthew and Luke both had a copy of Mark before them when they wrote, and incorporated large parts of it, though in different ways. This theory, known as the 'Priority of Mark', has been commonly regarded as one of the few assured results of critical scholarship. Some recent attempts to reassert the priority of Matthew in some form[1] have not yet won general acceptance, even if some of the points made carry conviction. They may result in a refinement of the commonly accepted view, but not in its total reversal. In the opinion of the overwhelming majority of scholars the priority of Mark remains the basis of synoptic studies.

However, another significant fact emerges out of the study of the synoptic texts in parallel columns: two hundred or so verses *not* found in Mark occur in both Matthew and Luke with striking verbal similarities. It seems unlikely that Luke copied from Matthew, or vice versa, since there is no instance (subsequent to the Temptation narrative) in which they insert this common material into the Marcan framework at the same point. The suggestion that they used a common store of unwritten tradition hardly commends itself since it does not account for the remarkable *verbal* agreements. So the explanation is offered that Matthew and Luke both used a common written source in addition to

Mark, a source once existing but now lost. This source is labelled 'Q'. So we reach what is called the 'Two Document Hypothesis'. Here it is important to be cautious. The existence of 'Q' has recently been called in question, e.g. by Dr Austin Farrer. Even if most scholars remain unconvinced by Dr Farrer's arguments, 'Q' remains a hypothesis (nobody has ever seen it!), and attempts to 'reconstruct' it are unimpressive. For practical purposes, however, the 'Q' hypothesis still stands, though not quite so steady on its feet as formerly. And even if it should entirely lose its balance, this would not radically alter the main tendency of synoptic study.

Returning to the study of texts in parallel columns, it next appears that both Matthew and Luke contain much material that is peculiar to each gospel, and not found elsewhere. There is the 'special Matthean material' (designated M), and the 'special Lucan' material (L). Whether these represent written sources, or oral traditions, or a bit of both, is a matter of debate among scholars, hardly affecting our present purposes. The point is that, in addition to Mark and 'Q', Matthew and Luke each use a source of material unknown to, or unused by, the other. Now even if this general view stands in need of some refinement, the really vital point to grasp is that the synoptic gospels contain several strands of material which can to an extent be distinguished. This discovery is of enormous importance in helping us to understand what kind of books the gospels are, for two reasons. 1. We are now able to see Matthew and Luke as the editors of a source already known to us, viz. Mark. Therefore, we can observe how they handle it, and thus see what kind of value and significance they attach to it. 2. We are enabled to compare together at least four independent sources, and thus to ask whether they are in basic agreement, or whether one stands in contradiction to another, or whether important elements appear in one and not another. Two important conclusions emerge out of these considerations, one negative and one positive.

The *negative* conclusion is that the two later evangelists

handle their Marcan source with remarkable freedom. They pay little attention to the order, and often replace it by their own. They do not scruple to alter or modify the details. As any modern commentary will show, they often expand and develop the material in order to give it relevance to the ongoing life and theology of the Church. Therefore, whatever their books may be, they are not like modern biographies, and their meaning is distorted if they are so treated. The *positive* conclusion is that, when all the various strands are compared, it becomes plain that Jesus is consistently presented in supernatural terms as the Christ, and Son of God, as the one through whom God has acted to bring in the New Order in accordance with his age-long purposes revealed in the ancient scriptures. That is to say, a positive Christology is embedded in all the sources the evangelists are handling. By the time they come to write, the history of Jesus was already an interpreted history, and interpreted along similar lines.[2] There is no trace of any source which is non-Christological, i.e. which presents Jesus simply as a prophet or rabbi who taught general truths about religion without regard to his own person or vocation. The doctrine, therefore, is not imposed by the evangelists on a previously undoctrinal material, but is found in all the sources they use. Therefore it must go back to the earliest days of the Church, and at least until the time of Mark, our earliest written source.

Can we leave it there, and say that in Mark we have an ultimate, bed-rock historical source for discovering, partially no doubt, but accurately, the actual events of Jesus' life, together with the precise content of what he said, and in the way he said it? Is Mark dependent, more or less directly, on the personal reminiscences of individual eye-witnesses, such as Peter? It used to be thought so. It was the view of the British scholar, F. C. Burkitt,[3] and is sometimes referred to as the 'Marcan Hypothesis'. But already, in 1901, a devastating blow had been struck against the hypothesis by the German scholar, William Wrede, who in a book called *The Messianic Secret in the Gospels* argued that Mark's gospel, so far from being a straightforward historical record, is saturated by doctrinal interests, and so dominated by a particular view of Jesus' messiahship (different in the author's view from what Jesus taught), that the underlying history is wholly overlaid by such interests. This was bad enough for the 'Marcan Hypothesis', but the final death blow was to be delivered in 1919 by another German scholar, K. L. Schmidt, who in making a detailed examination of the structure of the gospel reached certain startling conclusions. These were to the effect that the gospel consists of a number of basic units (called 'pericopes'), which were already in existence (though unwritten), and which the author has strung together very loosely and with the smallest regard for any historical connection. These units are quite unlike paragraphs in a biography, since each one is self-contained, and can (indeed must) be read without historical reference to what precedes or follows. The links are supplied by the evangelist (or by his source where he uses groupings already made), and are quite artificial. The units are linked by similarity of topic, rather than chronology. We have already noticed that Matthew and Luke sit very loose to the Marcan order, and often change its connecting links. It now appears that they were justified. The chronological order in which they occurred had long been forgotten, and the links supplied by Mark are editorial and contrived, being dictated by motives other than biographical. They have been likened to beads strung loosely together.

The basic unit, then, of the gospel material is neither the completed book, nor the written or unwritten collections on which they may be based, but the single, self-contained 'pericope' or saying. When it further appears (as will be shown later) that these basic units show unmistakable signs of having been moulded into definite shapes and patterns, it becomes clear that they too have a history behind them. What other history can be suggested than their continuing use in the corporate life of the Church – its evangelism, its teaching of converts, its pastoral care, its liturgy and worship? Thus between the direct reminiscences of eye-witnesses and the first attempt to make written collections of them, there intrudes a whole process of oral tradition, itself dynamic and community-centred. The study of this process marks one of the latest stages of NT scholarship, and is sometimes referred to as the 'traditio-historical' method. Its basic presupposition, as this expression suggests, is that every gospel saying or episode is the outcome of a history in the tradition, and that the study of this history throws important light on its proper meaning and interpretation. Since an important part of this study concerns the forms or patterns in which the tradition is thought to have been moulded and transmitted, this particular element in the enterprise goes by the name of 'Form Criticism'. The expression is often used, however, in a wider and looser sense to cover the whole enterprise. Form Criticism was first used on the OT by the scholar Hermann Gunkel, and then on the gospels, most notably by the two giants of modern German scholarship, Rudolf Bultmann and Martin Dibelius. It is no exaggeration to say that their work has provided the main inspiration for all subsequent NT study in Germany and America. In England it was made known chiefly through the works of R. H. Lightfoot, though British scholarship as a whole has tended (unwarrantably perhaps?) to be somewhat suspicious of it, or rather half-hearted in its use of the method.

Now form criticism concerns itself with the study of the oral tradition lying behind the gospel narratives, and so deals principally with the independent 'pericopes' of which those narratives are largely composed. When these units are studied, both in themselves and in the context of other community traditions and folk-lore (Jewish and Hellenistic), certain broad classifications emerge. First there are the narratives called, variously, paradigms, or apothegms or pronouncement-stories. A typical example is the story of our Lord eating with the outcasts (Mark 2.15-17), or of the man with the withered hand (Mark 3.1-5). These consist of a notable saying of the Lord, surrounded by a short and simple narrative. The narrative is bald, lacking in interest, and often varies in detail from gospel to gospel. The saying tends to remain constant, and is clearly the focus of the episode. Seemingly the saying was remembered and transmitted carefully, while the narrative setting could be modified, or perhaps even invented sometimes, so as to throw the saying into greater relief. The pronouncement-story is a very definite form, and according to the critics, the earliest to take shape. The very baldness of the narrative has been taken to suggest that the episode had been so constantly in the Church's teaching that all unnecessary detail had dropped away in the interests of preserving the saying, the central gem. The episode had been rounded and made smooth by constant use, rather like a pebble made smooth by constant washing of the waves on the beach. All this is taken as evidence of regular *public* use by the Church, the entire interest being that of religious instruction, not biographical curiosity. As such these episodes bear, as it were, the 'imprimatur' of the earliest Church, and so have high claim to authenticity.

The second chief classification consists of the 'miracle stories' or 'novellen'. These also follow a fairly stereotyped pattern, but there is more detail, and the emphasis is on the wonderful works of the Lord, rather than the word which he speaks – though sometimes the two forms are mixed. Form critics suggest that these tales are not so firmly anchored in public teaching and worship. Their interest is less severely religious and practical. Wealth of detail is taken as a sign of the story-teller's art rather than the influence of eye-witness report. The general verdict is that, taken as a whole, they give an authentic generalized picture of the sort of thing that Jesus did (e.g. healing the sick, 'casting out devils'), but cannot be confidently relied on in detail, or in any particular instance.

The third classification consists in isolated sayings of the Lord, of various types, and extensive in scope. Then there are some other narratives, difficult to classify, such as the Baptism or Transfiguration of Jesus, which have no particular form but are characterized by their christological purpose and supernatural thrust. Then finally we have the Passion narratives. In contrast to the preceding narrative of the ministry, these are not a collection of independent units, but a connected whole, moving forward in intelligible chronological sequence. This is explained on the grounds that the Passion narrative was recited at length and written down at an early stage, before the normal laws of tradition history had time to operate. The reason for this is not hard to seek. The chief obstacle to the acceptance of the gospel, both among Jew and Greek, was the fact that the one who claimed to be Christ and Lord ended his life in ignominy on the gallows, accused of crimes against both Church and State. There was therefore an immediate need to recount the circumstances of his death in order to show (1) that he was innocent of these charges, and (2) that all that had happened was in accordance with the age-long purposes of God, and 'according to the scriptures'. Hence the unusual interest in detail, and the desire to tell a connected story, the elements of which are closely associated with certain OT passages (notably Psalm 22) which told of the innocent suffering of the Righteous One of God. When we move on to the Resurrection Narratives, things revert to normal, and we find again a series of loosely connected pericopes. For the resurrection did not present the same kind of difficulty in the Church's preaching, so that the need for a connected narrative did not at first arise.

The essential contribution of this whole line of approach is to make it clear that the words and works of Jesus, as they have come down to us, owe their survival and present form to their use in the gatherings of the early Christian communities for religious purposes. This does *not* mean that they are for this reason necessarily unhistorical or 'invented' (see chapter 7). But their creative milieu, their setting in life (*Sitz im Leben*, to use the German phrase), was the communal life of the Church in all its varied forms. There is some disagreement among scholars about which of the Church's activities contributed most to the formation of the tradition. Some emphasize the apologetic need (i.e. to defend the Christian claims against misunderstanding and calumny), others emphasize the preaching of the gospel, others the teaching of converts, others the liturgical and sacramental activities. This does not affect the central point, that the predominant interests in preserving and transmitting the 'things concerning Jesus' were religious, theological, practical. For example, the Church was interested in transmitting what Jesus had said about paying tribute to Caesar, because the 'Church and State' problem was real to them. They were not interested, however, in preserving biographical notes about the precise circumstances in which he said it. They were vitally interested in the *fact* that Jesus was the Christ, but not at all in the precise stages in which Jesus himself did or did not come to a full realization of it. We may be deeply interested in such matters, but the gospels were not written to satisfy *our* historical curiosity. Basically, each pericope is a kind of sermon outline, intended to bring out the significance for faith and morals of some word or deed of Jesus: they are not at all like the connected paragraphs of a modern biography. The episodes of the gospel tradition were formed, preserved and developed in order to throw light on what faith in Christ crucified and risen really meant in relation to the problems, needs and conflicts of the present. Biographical concern, and interest in the past as such, was strictly subservient to this aim. One must read the gospels through the eyes and minds of the early Christian community in whose setting they were formed, if one is to hope to understand what they have to say.

A number of important implications follow:

1. By asking of each pericope what is the setting in life which appears best to fit it and explain it, we are in a position to approach the gospel material on three levels, and ask: (*a*) What did this mean for the evangelist and his readers, and therefore what am I invited to make of it as it stands? (*b*) What did it mean in the process of transmission which preceded its incorporation in the written gospel? (*c*) What did it mean on the lips of Jesus, if indeed his words are in any degree recoverable? Scholars such as C. H. Dodd and

Joachim Jeremias have submitted the parables to this kind of study with remarkable results. By using their methods it is often possible to recover with reasonable confidence the original significance of a parable as Jesus spoke it, and to compare this with the version which has emerged in our gospels as a result of its later use and adaptation in the tradition. This, of course, raises a whole host of questions which must be left for a separate chapter.

2. The gospels are now seen to be essentially community productions. This does not mean that the evangelists made no vital contribution, as the next chapter will show. But it does mean that we are released from bothering too much about matters of date and authorship, as people once did. The authority behind the gospels is that of the community, not only of the individual evangelists.

3. We are allowed to approach each gospel episode on its own, and to recognize that it has no necessary historical connection with what precedes or follows it in the narrative. Now it must first be admitted that this imposes severe limits on what we can hope to know about the 'life of Jesus' as this phrase is normally understood. For if we do not know the order in which the events occurred, we cannot hope to answer such questions as interest the biographer, e.g. how the thought of Jesus developed about his ministry and destiny, or the internal constitution of his mind. But this limitation, once accepted, proves a point of release and advance, in two directions: (a) We are released from the need to explain each gospel episode on the assumption that it must have a historical connection with what precedes and follows. Many a preacher has wrestled with the problem of how to interpret the parable of the Man without a Wedding Garment, in the context of the parable of the Marriage Feast in which it is found. How could the poor fellow be expected to have had a wedding garment, when he had just been dragged there by the scruff of his neck from the highways and hedges? How unfair that he should be cast into outer darkness! All sorts of desperate expedients have been used to solve this one, including the invention of an 'ancient

37

custom' of giving out wedding garments in the entrance hall! The problem immediately disappears when it is realized that here we have two parables, spoken by Jesus on separate occasions, which the evangelist has put together on grounds of similarity of subject-matter. So all attempts to find a historical connection between the episodes in a gospel, still more to 'harmonize' the events of the various gospels with one another, are now seen to be a complete waste of time. And that is a great relief for the interpreter. (b) The refusal to find such historical connections enables us to ask the really relevant question: of what kind *are* these connections? Often they are pretty arbitrary, but often they can easily be shown to be *theological*. That is to say, the order of events in the narrative is often controlled by a concern to interpret the meaning of these events for faith. Theological truth is conveyed not only by the narratives, but also by the order in which these narratives are presented. This discovery has proved a notable advance in a true and relevant exegesis of the gospel texts. Nowhere does this appear more clearly than in the central part of Mark's gospel.[4] Here we have a story of a gradual *physical* enlightenment (the blind man), which finds its commentary in the subsequent story of gradual *spiritual* enlightenment (Peter's confession of Jesus' Messiahship). Then this story is commented on in the ensuing narrative of the Transfiguration, followed immediately by the first prediction of the Passion. The significance of these juxtapositions is clearly seen in the light of Mark's doctrine of Christ, who enters into his glory not in spite of but because of his suffering and death, and whose true Messiahship must, therefore, be partially hidden this side of the passion and resurrection. The order of episodes in this central section of the gospel is of great significance, but that which controls it is not history but doctrine.

4. Now that we are made aware of what the gospels are *not*, we are in a better position to understand what kind of books they are, and what they are good for. A careful study of them leads to the remarkable conclusion that they do not

fit into any known 'genre' of literature, ancient or modern. This statement is based on strictly scientific and historical judgments. But to the eye of faith it will not seem at all strange. How could the coming of God incarnate fail to produce a brand new type of literature, as unique as the event it records? Since the Word was made *flesh*, the literature was bound to be more than a piece of natural reportage, but rather shot through at every point by a transcendent reference. The primary purpose of the gospels is to show that the Christian claim that Jesus is the Son of God is a true claim, and to throw light on the meaning of his person and work by reference to certain selected elements of his human career. This is done partly by setting these elements against the background of the OT, so as to show that in him God's promise to bring in the new age is fulfilled. It is also done by presenting the human career of Jesus through the prism of the Easter faith in him, as the living Lord of the Church, and the source and goal of a new humanity. It must never be forgotten that the one of whom the evangelists wrote was the one whom they and their readers worshipped Sunday by Sunday as the living Lord, through whom God had acted for the world's salvation. That is why the gospel episodes are more like sermon outlines than sections in a biography. That is why these episodes are not like dry bits of wood waiting for the faith of the reader to light them up, but are already ablaze with the faith of those who had participated in them. History and interpretation, fact and symbol, are interwoven throughout. This is not for one moment to say that the gospels give us a false or distorted picture of the one who stands behind these records – of that more in a later chapter. It is to say with all possible emphasis that the records are aimed not at satisfying the historical curiosity of the modern reader, but at evoking and deepening faith in Jesus as Lord. We are offered not the record of a dead and gone teacher whose words had carefully to be preserved just as they stood, but rather an account of the impact of the 'things concerning Jesus' on that community which found in him the source of a new life, a life which they believed came straight from God, and was the true life for every man. In the words of Professor Knox, it is 'Jesus-in-the-midst-of-his-own' that we are given, and that both *before* and even more compellingly *after* his death. What Professor C. F. Evans says in connection with the Lord's Prayer and the Lord's Supper can really be applied to the entire gospel record. 'We may not know exactly and verbatim what Jesus said and did, because we now have it refracted through the experience of those who, by using what he said and did, had come to appreciate more of what he was to them.'[5]

NOTES

1. B. C. Butler, *The Originality of St Matthew* (1951); Pierson Parker, *The Gospel before Mark* (1953); W. R. Farmer, *The Synoptic Problem* (1964).

2. E. C. Hoskyns and N. Davey, *The Riddle of the New Testament* (1931), chapter 7.

3. F. C. Burkitt, *The Gospel History and its Transmission* (1906).

4. Mark 8.22–9.32.

5. C. F. Evans, *The Lord's Prayer* (1963), p. 12.

4 Gospel Writers

Just as Judaism was a living community governed by a common memory, chiefly the Exodus, which had called that community into being and still exercised a decisive power in its worship and life, so the Christian Church looked back to an event which called it into being and continued to exercise a creative influence on its worship, witness and life. This event was the whole career of Jesus, focused upon his death and resurrection, by virtue of which the one who was remembered was also experienced as a living and universal presence. In the last chapter we traced the stages by which this memory was preserved, between the direct reminiscences of the eye-witnesses to the production of the synoptic gospels. This has led us to the view that the evangelists were not 'original authors' in the modern sense, but rather compilers of material which had behind it a history of development in the communal life of the early Church. Yet in another sense they were very creatively original. They were not mere hacks, contributing nothing of their own to the total witness to Christ. The material they handled was not original, but their handling of it most certainly was.

The Gospel according to St Mark (usually dated between AD 65 and AD 70) was written against a background of *conflict* and *persecution*. It is of sufficiently early a date to reflect the tremendous difficulty the early Church experienced in preaching a suffering rather than a triumphant Messiah, and in persuading would-be converts that to belong to the Messianic community meant a share in suffering before it would mean a participation in glory. The author therefore must wrestle with the paradox that the Messiah, when he

41

appeared, was rejected by his own people, and ended his life in a shameful death, deserted by friends and foes alike. So his gospel is especially aimed at showing that the sufferings of Jesus were not only innocent but the divinely appointed means whereby he entered into his glory, and became God's agent in salvation. The Passion casts its shadow over the whole narrative right from the beginning. The early stories of controversy foreshadow and seek to explain the final denouement of the conflict which brought Jesus to his inevitable end. The selection of parables which Mark has chosen to record present the basic theme that God's kingdom, or reign, must be hidden before it can be revealed. The whole of the second half of the gospel consists of an extended sermon on the way of the cross, first for the Christ and then for his disciples. It is true that Jesus is also represented as a figure of supreme authority, both in the words he speaks and the mighty deeds he performs. But the emphatic and constant commands to keep these things secret (best understood as an editorial device rather than a historical reminiscence) make clear to the reader that *these* in themselves are not the grounds on which any claim to glory is to be based. Only *after* the Passion, and in the light of the Easter faith, can the wonderful works of the earthly Jesus be properly interpreted. It is as if Mark were saying to his readers: 'Yes, Jesus is indeed the Christ and Son of God. He always has been, before as well as after the resurrection. But he is this, not because he possessed certain supernatural powers, after the fashion of a Jewish sorcerer or a Hellenistic wonder-worker. He is this because of his perfect obedience to a divine destiny, because of his perfect willingness to give himself a ransom for many, even to the point of the death on the Cross. Therefore to speak of Christ's glory, or even to speak of him as Christ at all, before or apart from his Passion is so misleading as to be positively untrue. And because *this* is the kind of Messiah he is, his disciples must not be surprised if they are called to a like destiny, and discover for themselves the same pattern of glory.' In fact Mark is saying very much the same thing that Paul says so often in his letters. Paul speaks of God commending his own love to us in that, while we were yet sinners, Christ died for us; and he claims that it is the destiny of Christians to be crucified with Christ, in order that they may be raised with him to newness of life. The only difference is that Paul says this in terms of theological concepts, whereas Mark does so in the form of a narrative, and by the way he handles and edits the community traditions concerning Jesus. The main point to grasp is that Mark's use of the traditional material is governed by some particular aims, these aims deriving directly from the particular situation (of conflict, etc.) in which the community for which he wrote found itself. Mark, then, is a theologian in his own right, who makes a distinctive contribution to that growing understanding of the meaning of Christ in the early days of the Church, of which the NT is the completed record.

The Gospel according to St Matthew (usually dated *circa* AD 90) was written from a situation of *consolidation*. Therefore his use of the material is fuller, less selective, more comprehensive. The pogrom of the Emperor Nero against the Christians, which may well have influenced the writing of Mark, was localized and short-lived. The Church for which Matthew wrote, in a different place and at a later date, though in conflict with contemporary Judaism, was not dominated by the threat of immediate or bloody persecution, and was living a more settled life. So the author is interested in preserving and adapting a much broader area of the tradition; indeed, he seems to want to include as much as he can, so that his work might become definitive. Moreover, the end of the world, which in the earlier period represented by Mark was thought of as being 'any minute now', was no longer expected so soon. To be sure, Matthew is specially interested in the details and 'staging' of it, in a way comparatively foreign both to the teaching of Jesus and to the earliest tradition. But now it is expected that there will also be a delay, and therefore a period of *waiting*. If then the Church must settle down to a period of waiting, then clearly it must consolidate its own life, and plan for its mission to proclaim the gospel to all the nations. So we are not surprised to find both these interests dominating Matthew's gospel, to such an extent that it is sometimes called the 'ecclesiastical gospel'. The period of waiting might be limited, but it was to be filled with a positive content. Now this 'ecclesiastical' interest is found clearly in those sections which deal with Church order and discipline (ch. 18), and in the passages which deal with the authority of Peter and the apostles (especially 16.18–19). It comes out even more strongly in the final paragraph, where words are placed upon the lips of the Risen Lord which in fact reflect the Church's developed conviction about its nature and mission. 'Go therefore and make disciples of all nations, baptizing them in the name of the Father and of the Son and of the Holy Spirit, teaching them to observe all that I have commanded you; and, lo, I am with you always, to the close of the age.' But this concern for consolidating the life of the Church is found much more pervasively in the way in which the words of Jesus are subtly adjusted and adapted so as to give direct guidance to a committed congregation. Words originally spoken to a partly indifferent, partly hostile audience, by way of a challenge to decision, are here modified into a kind of manual of instruction for the edification of the faithful.

Matthew's Christ, then, is not only the one who gives his life a ransom for many, and nerves his followers to share his own conflicts and sufferings; he is also the Lord of a community to which he is related both as ruler and teacher. He shows to the members of this community the true 'righteousness', the true way of life in relation to God, which will qualify them for the life of the age to come. This tendency to stress the role of Christ as the giver of a new Law is doubtless connected with the fact that the Church for which Matthew wrote was predominantly Jewish in composition, and that Matthew himself was almost certainly a converted Jew, possibly a converted rabbi. So the Christian Church in this gospel is *par excellence* the new Israel, and Jesus the one who provides it with a Law, like a new Moses. More precisely, Jesus is the second Moses who brings the only true and authentic interpretation of the old Law to be the basis of that 'righteousness' which is to exceed that of the scribes and Pharisees, whose interpretations are now superseded. The Christ of this gospel is not only the Redeemer but also the once humiliated but now exalted King, the giver of a new 'righteousness' to his people, among whom he is even now present in power, and who will come again in glory as universal Judge and Saviour. He is, in short, the Lord of all Life. The gospel, therefore, turns out to be a full, compendious handbook of instruction for the Messianic community, eagerly awaiting the fulfilment of its hopes, but in the meantime concerned with the consolidating of its life, worship and mission in the world.

The Gospel according to St Luke (usually dated between AD 80 and AD 90) was written from a situation of *expansion*. The Church for which Luke wrote was not faced with active, organized persecution, nor did it appear to be expecting an imminent, or even somewhat delayed, end of the world. Rather, the author appears to envisage an indefinite period of human history, which is to be characterized by the expansion of the Church, under the present guidance of the Spirit of the exalted Christ, until it embraces all humanity, Jew and Gentile, bond and free. Hence alone of the evangelists Luke continues his story (itself carefully dated in terms of secular history)[1] beyond the resurrection, and adds a second volume, Acts, in which he traces the triumphant expansion of the Christian movement until it is established in the very heart of the civilized world, Rome. He is dependent, in the writing of his gospel, on exactly the same kind of oral and written material as were Mark and Matthew. But his treatment of them has been subtly yet decisively altered by reason of the wider perspective from which he writes. The life, death and resurrection of Jesus are no longer presented as the *end* of history (as in Mark, and, with reservations, in Matthew), but as the *centre* of history. The period of Christ's coming has been preceded by a period of preparation, and is to be succeeded by a further period in

45

which age-long barriers are to be thrown down and a new world-wide community comes to birth. Thus the gospel begins with the story of the infant Jesus, who in the fullness of the time is proclaimed to be the light who is to lighten the *Gentiles*. The book of Acts begins and ends on exactly the same note, and is dominated by a like interest. The kindness of Jesus towards the outcasts (tax-collectors, sinners, Samaritans) with which the gospel is full, fore-shadows the universal mission of the Church to break down all barriers of race, culture and colour, and bring all humanity into one. The controlling element in this process is no longer the Mosaic Law, but the Spirit of God which replaces it and which is poured out on men of all nations. Within this perspective the death of Jesus is somewhat differently conceived. It is indeed of divine appointment, but is no longer presented as an act of atonement ushering in the speedy end of history. Rather it is, in the first place, a necessary transition from an earthly (and therefore limited) existence to a heavenly, and therefore universal existence – so that Jesus of Nazareth becomes the exalted Christ who governs the life and mission of the Church through the Spirit. Secondly, it is the supreme manifestation of that all-embracing charity, forgiveness and patience under suffering, which is to win men to faith and repentance, and thus inform the life of the Church. The Christ who meets us in these pages is depicted as *par excellence* the friend of publicans and sinners in his earthly life, precisely because he is to become the source of universal community through the continuing work of his Spirit within the ongoing life of the Church catholic.

Two conclusions now emerge:

1. The synoptic gospels give three complementary but distinct portraits of Jesus. They are complementary in that they deal with the same general sequence of events, spring out of the same basic experience of the living Lord in his Church, and share in a common body of tradition. They are distinct in that each is intended to be read in its own right rather than by reference to the others, and also in that each

is related to differing backgrounds, needs and interests. An important corollary arises for interpretation. It is obvious that a mountain presents a very different set of impressions according to the perspective from which it is viewed. If, therefore, you want to have a pictorial record of it, you must possess several pictures of it taken from different angles. But then it is no use at all just superimposing them one upon another in the hope of producing a single whole; that way you only produce a smudge! So with the gospels, it is no use just ignoring the distinctiveness of each portrait by seeking to harmonize them one with the other, or you reduce them all to a shapeless pulp. To take but one example, in Mark the last words of Jesus from the cross are, 'My God, my God, why hast thou forsaken me?'; whereas in Luke his last words are, 'Father, into thy hands I commend my spirit'. Now it is quite improper to join these two together and suppose that Jesus said them both one after the other, presumably with a change of mood in between. The fact is that we simply have no means of knowing what were the last words of Jesus. What we have to do is to interpret each saying within the context of the particular purposes of the gospel in which it is found, recognizing that both sayings belong to a finished and distinctive portrait rather than to some undifferentiated and exact photographic record. Mark's purpose is to stress the total dereliction in which Jesus fulfilled his destiny, and the completeness of his identification with the human tragedy. Luke's concern is to emphasize the invincibility of his faith and his love. The reconciliation of these two interpretations of the death of Christ belongs to systematic theology rather than to biblical criticism. What, then, do you do with your several pictures of that mountain drawn from different angles? Surely you look at each in turn, allow each separate presentation to sink into your mind and imagination, and only then may you get an impression of the whole. So it is with the study of the gospels. We must allow each gospel to bear its own witness to Christ. When we have done this we become aware that it is recognizably the same figure who stands behind them

47

all. But the portrait which each one points is different. We have no direct access to 'Jesus in himself', if we may so speak, but instead three presentations of the *impact* which he made, and continued to make. And these impacts are not the same, because the people on whom they were made differed in their circumstances, needs, backgrounds, ways of thinking, and manner of response. The three interpretations of Christ are complementary, but not uniform. They present not one, but three types of theology.

2. All the gospels were written against the common background of faith in Christ *crucified and risen.* Those who wrote and those who heard them presupposed this faith. And this made all the difference to the way they told their tale and handled their historical material. The implications of this will be considered in a subsequent chapter. Here it is sufficient to note that the evangelists, for all their wealth of detail in recounting the words and works of the earthly Jesus, thought of him always as identical with the present and living Lord of their own experience; and that therefore their basic interest lay at the same point as it does in the writings of Paul and the other NT theologians, viz. in the proclamation of the faith of Christ, crucified and risen.

If we keep these considerations in mind we shall not be surprised when, on turning to the epistles of Paul, we begin to breathe an atmosphere which appears outwardly very different from that of the gospels, only to discover that it really belongs to very much the same climate.

NOTE

1. Luke 3.1–2.

5 Paul

Before picking up the theme of the previous chapter, we must first pause to consider briefly the kind of literature we are dealing with in the epistles of Paul. The central importance of these writings in our understanding of the NT is self-evident. They are the earliest written documents, they are autobiographical, and of the authenticity of many there can be no reasonable doubt (see appendix). They were written at the same time that the gospel tradition was taking shape. We do, in fact, possess another source for our knowledge of the life of Paul, namely the account given in the book of Acts. This, however, must be treated with some caution. The author of Acts has some very strong apologetic motives in writing, and these have led him to idealize somewhat the course of events. Acts is history, but in the ancient rather than the modern sense. Moreover, it was written considerably later than the events recorded – probably around AD 80–90, though a few scholars regard it as a second-century production. Even if it was written by a companion of Paul (and this may well be doubted), it seems unlikely that he was a very close companion, otherwise it is difficult to explain why he is so little affected by the distinctive ideas of the apostle, and seems to be ignorant of his letters. Certainly we may justifiably supplement our knowledge about Paul from the pages of Acts, but must always give preference to Paul's own account of things when, as sometimes happens, it runs counter to the impressions derived from the second-hand, and somewhat biased, records of Acts. In any case we have in that collection of letters whose authenticity is undisputed, an impressive amount of first-hand material on which a study of the thought and outlook of the apostle may be based.

It is also important to understand what kind of a document an 'epistle' really is, so that we may know how to handle and interpret it. In the ancient world there existed two types of literature to which the word 'epistle' was applied. There were genuine letters, in the ordinary sense, written to individuals or groups, whose purpose was to communicate advice or information about particular matters of common concern to writer and reader. There were also 'epistles' of a different type, whose object was not to effect communication with any particular person or persons in relation to a concrete situation, but rather to provide a treatise or sermon on some general subject. Though in the form of letters, they were not the sort of document which you would put in an envelope and send through the post. A much closer modern parallel would be the 'open letter' in *The Times* newspaper. Now Paul's 'epistles' appear to be a mixture of these two types. On the one hand they are genuine correspondence, written to deal with particular concerns to particular groups of people. Some of the subjects dealt with are in connection with controversies of great moment in the life of the contemporary Church: e.g., Must people first become Jews before they can become Christians? What constitutes church unity? What happens when we die? Others are provided by certain practical concerns, like the collection which Paul is organizing for the impoverished Christians at Jerusalem, or how public worship should be ordered. Yet even the most severely practical, or even trivial, of these concerns are constantly related to one or other of the great theological truths which Paul is above all else anxious to convey. Even his rather quaint advice to women about wearing hats in church is related (to our minds somewhat unfortunately) to the doctrine of man made in the image of God. Again, it was the fact that the Christians at Corinth were inclined to make pigs of themselves and get a little drunk at the Lord's Supper which occasioned some of the most profound teaching on the eucharist and on the nature of community to be found anywhere in the NT. So it is that Paul's letters have the quality of theological treatises (Romans in particular), and thus form an admixture of the two types of 'epistle' mentioned above.

But there is another factor which lends to this literature its distinctive flavour, and that is the note of authority with which the author writes. He passionately believes himself to be an *apostle*, that is to say, one with a direct commission from the risen Lord to act as his accredited agent. Moreover, the letters are addressed, not to any private individual, or collection of individuals, but to 'the church' in this place or that. Thus both the call of the author and the dignity of the recipients give to these writings that distinctive quality and strong whiff of authority which might justify us in preferring the old-fashioned word 'epistle' to describe them, rather than the colourless word 'letter'. Moreover, in spite of their occasional character and origin, they may properly be called theological writings, so long as it is understood that the theology for the most part springs directly out of the occasions with which they deal, and therefore is not systematic.

Now it is a central theme of this book that the NT contains no uniform theology, but contains a number of differing and distinctive interpretations of the event of Christ in relation to the community which grew up around it. So now we return to this central theme by drawing the reader's attention at this stage to the highly distinctive and profound contribution which is peculiar to Paul, and not just simply uniform with other theologies whether earlier, contemporary, or later. Paul himself is not afraid to refer to this distinctive element as '*my* gospel'. Now this distinctiveness is partly due to the fact that Paul's background and experience were wider than that of the original apostles from whose testimony earliest Christianity was derived. He shared with them Jewish birth and descent, but was unlike them in three respects. 1. He had been brought up very strictly within the Pharisaic tradition in Judaism, being schooled in the outlook and methods of the Rabbis. 2. He had come into close contact with Hellenistic culture, by virtue of being a native of Tarsus, a very cosmopolitan city. 3. He appears to have been a citizen of the Roman Empire, and proud of it. All these factors would tend to give his understanding of the gospel a wider range.

Yet all this is as nothing compared with the influence on his theology of his own 'conversion', so different was it from the way the original apostles had come to faith. The word 'conversion' has been put in quotation marks, because it is a rather misleading term to use in Paul's case. His 'conversion' was *not* a change from one religion to another, for he continued to worship the same God, and use the same sacred scriptures after it as before. It was *not* a conversion from a life of sin to one of virtue, as in the classic Salvation Army instances. It was *not* the result of evangelistic preaching, as in a Billy Graham Crusade. Nor is there sufficient evidence for the view, often advanced, that it came at the end of an inward moral struggle or a conscious sense of guilt, as in the case of Luther. An unbiased reading of such passages as Phil. 3.6 precludes such views. What, then, were the particular features which distinguished Paul's experience of Christ from that of the other apostles?

First, it took the form of an encounter with the *risen* Christ – sudden, surprising, and unrepeated. As Paul puts it, it pleased God 'to reveal his Son in me'. It is true that the other apostles laid claim to their apostolic authority by virtue of their direct witness to the resurrection; but they had already known Jesus in the flesh, and been his disciples. But Paul became both a Christian and an apostle without having first been a disciple. This might account for his relative indifference to the earthly life and teaching of Jesus. It certainly helps to explain his devouring interest in the meaning of the *death* of Christ, and its centrality in his theology; for the Christ he came to know was essentially the one whom God had raised from the *dead*. Moreover, the very unexpectedness of his call (a better term to use than 'conversion'), and the total reversal of values to which it led him, would account for the way Paul represents faith in

Christ as an utterly radical redirection, indeed a 'new creation'.

Secondly, not only was Paul not a disciple when he received his call, he was actually a bitter opponent of the Christian movement. He was called to be a Christian, even more, an apostle, in the very act of persecuting the followers of the one who called him. This would account for the enormous emphasis in his theology on the notion of *grace* – that is to say, the incredible and unconditional mercy of God in Christ towards all men, quite irrespective of their merits. This precisely was what Paul experienced with stabbing immediacy on the Damascus road. It explains his conviction that Christ is the 'end of the law' to those who believe. It explains, or partly explains, why Paul thought of himself from the moment of his Call as one with a special mission to the *Gentiles*, i.e. to those who most of all were 'outsiders' when it came to knowledge of and obedience to the Law. For if God offered his mercy without any reference to human merit (as he had done to Paul, the arch-enemy of his purposes), then the attempt to achieve it 'by the works of the Law', was ruled out of court, and with it disappeared any distinction between Jew and Gentile.

Thirdly, Paul came to Christian faith after first having been a Pharisee, i.e. one whose entire religion was based on the conviction that the way to receive God's favour was by obedience to his Law, with the utmost zeal and the most meticulous detail. This is the reason why Paul felt compelled to persecute the Church with such fanaticism. For these Christians claimed as Messiah one who had suffered the kind of shameful death which placed him under the curse of the Law itself, so that to confess this man as Messiah was to call in question the absolute validity of the Law itself. That was bad enough. But even worse was the blasphemous effrontery of the Christians in claiming that God had sent his Messiah to *them*, of all people. Just look at them! Of all men the least deserving of God's favour! They were drawn from the ranks of the common people of Palestine who, while assenting to the Law of God, were ignorant of its real requirements, and moreover quite unable, by virtue of their daily occupation, to fulfil its difficult ritual demands, especially those which prohibited any dealings with Gentiles, at least without elaborate purifications afterwards. These were the 'tax collectors and sinners', real irresponsible riff-raff, the folk referred to disparagingly in Pharisaic circles as 'the people of the land'! And they had the sheer nerve to believe that God's Messiah had been sent to *them*, rather than to the loyal and conscientious churchmen of the day. So Paul the Pharisee was faced with an immense challenge. Either they were wrong, in which case theirs was the final blasphemy. Or they were right, in which case everything which Paul had believed about God's ways with man was turned upside down. What happened on the Damascus road suddenly convinced Paul that they were right. It followed then that what truly leads men to God is not their pious deeds, not their spiritual achievements, but simply the unmerited grace of God offered freely to those who least of all deserved it, but who were ready to receive it as a gift. Paul's understanding of God's ways with men was turned upside down. That is obvious. What is not so often perceived is that the thing which occasioned this change was Paul's *encounter with the Church*.[1] Paul is quite certain that the agent of his 'conversion' was Jesus Christ. Yet there is no evidence that the life of the historic Jesus had any direct influence on the apostle; rather the contrary. But the essence of Jesus' gospel and the outcome of his life's work was found in the actual constitution of his Church – the despised, the tax-collectors and sinners, the weary and heavy-laden – and it was his encounter with *this* community which formed the raw material of his conversion to Christ, and his subsequent understanding of Christ. Paul was not converted *by* the Church, but he was most certainly converted *through* the Church, and *into* the Church. *This* comes out clearly in the conversion stories themselves, where it is asserted that in persecuting *Christians* Paul was actually persecuting Christ himself.

Here, then, in these various factors which led up to Paul's

call, we have all the ingredients in his own distinctive theology, in what he calls 'my gospel': the great doctrine of justification by faith, of salvation through grace; the great wrestlings with the meaning of the cross, with all the master images of victory, redemption, expiation, etc.; the passionate sense of an apostolate to the gentile world; the conviction that in Christ all barriers between Jew and Gentile, and with them all other barriers too, are once and for all thrown down.

It would, however, be the greatest possible mistake to draw the conclusion that Paul's 'gospel' consists in certain 'ideas' or 'doctrines', however profound. The attempt, for example, to interpret Paul – or even worse, Christianity – purely on the basis of the doctrine of justification by faith, normally understood in an individualistic sense, and taken in isolation, leads to a cul-de-sac. For behind such propositions as this there lies a concrete experience so rich and variegated as to defy definition in any form of words or concepts. The precise characteristics of the experience will vary considerably according to the particular background and previous life of the recipient. In Paul's case, as we have seen, this was of such a kind as to express itself quite naturally in such a doctrine as justification by grace through faith. This conveyed its special flavour. But again, as we have seen, that impact of Christ upon him, which crystallized out into this particular doctrine, was quite inseparable from his encounter with the Christian community, so that for him as for his fellow Christians the saving knowledge of Christ was never to be dissociated from participation in the corporate life of the community, and in this context alone made any sense.

Two important corollaries follow. First, it becomes necessary to emphasize that, for all its distinctiveness, Paul's theology is deeply rooted in the concrete experience and on-going life of the Christian community. Indeed, his theology is genuinely new, a really fresh departure; and it often brings him into collision with some of the more conservative elements in the contemporary Church. But Paul himself is a 'churchman' through and through, and certainly no free-lance evangelist or philosopher. It must be remembered that his epistles are pastoral rather than evangelistic, so that he constantly presupposes the basic experience of the Church, and of the 'kerygma' in which it was first expressed. This he shares with his readers. Again, he often shows himself to be dependent on the tradition of the Church, and sometimes quotes or alludes to parts of it. He 'delivers' what he has himself 'received'.[2] He quotes from traditional hymns and credal formulae. He draws upon the remembered words of Jesus, though indirectly. He shares in the general understanding of the sacrament of baptism, and himself participates in the eucharist. He includes in his letters sections from ethical codes, themselves taken over from Jewish and Hellenistic sources. Not only is Paul thus dependent on tradition, he also contributes to it, in that some of his original ideas later become common property in the Church. For example, both the Gospel of Mark and the Gospel of John seem to have been influenced, directly or indirectly, by Pauline theology.

The second corollary is that the highly personal elements in Paul's theology, summed up in the doctrine of 'justification by faith', need to be balanced by, and integrated with, all that he has to say about being 'in the Spirit', or 'in Christ', or being made members of the 'Body of Christ' . . . that is to say, living a new kind of community existence, initiated by baptism, nourished by the eucharist, and governed by that Holy Spirit which is inseparable from the presence of the risen Christ in the midst of his own. In other words, the distinctive elements in Paul's theology are woven on to a very broad tapestry, whose basic theme concerns God's grand design to fashion a new human community out of the old. The old humanity (man apart from faith, the 'old Adam') is hopelessly estranged from its true nature as created in the image of God. It is a prey to that basic anxiety or faithlessness from which all actual deeds of evil spring. Out of this old humanity God has brought into being the 'new man', freed from the compulsion to prove his own worth, because he now relies on God's loving acceptance of him; freed, therefore, from anxiety, greed and pride; reconciled with himself, with his neighbour (even the least deserving), with his universe, and thus with God. The instrument which God used to effect this transition, this 'new creation', was 'Jesus Christ our Lord', himself the 'new Adam', the fount and source of a newly constituted human race. God had thus called into being a new humanity by raising Jesus the crucified from the dead. Out of the dying of Jesus on the cross God had brought into being a human race restored to its true nature. This new humanity thus takes the form of the Christian community, the Church. In this community the existence of the new humanity is partially but truly realized . . . or better, is in process of realization. Though a minority among men, it is potentially and in intention coterminous with the whole human race. Part of its function and destiny is so to act and so to live that all men everywhere may come to a true realization of themselves, so finding peace and reconciliation. Such is the great design which Paul weaves on to his theological tapestry. It is not surprising, then, that in his most exalted moments Paul envisages the ultimate reconciliation of all things and all men; and the thought so ravishes his heart that he cries exultantly: 'O the depth of the riches and wisdom and knowledge of God! How unsearchable are his judgments and how inscrutable his ways!' (Rom. 11.33.)

In conclusion, it may be useful to see how all this relates to the central thesis of this book. We have argued that the matrix out of which the whole NT springs is the experienced reality of the Church's community life, in all its positive distinctiveness, that this experienced reality is inseparable from the continuing impact of the 'event of Jesus Christ', an impact so strong that the Jesus who is remembered is experienced as a living and universal presence; and that this interpretation of present experience and remembered event constantly seeks expression, both in sacramental acts, and in a spoken message or profession of faith. Now all this would seem to be pre-eminently true in the case of the writings of Paul. 1. For all the intensely personal character of his call or conversion, it 'was encounter with the Christian community which occasioned it; and its validity was tested by and found expression in Paul's experience of 'life in Christ Jesus', that is to say the distinctive experience of reconciliation within the community of believers, the Body of Christ. 2. Yet this experience of the apostle was quite inseparable from his conviction that it was through Jesus Christ that God effected this work of reconciliation. His experience of the new life in the Spirit was dominated and controlled by his understanding of the event of Christ, especially at its central point of death and resurrection. To put it in another way: Paul is interested in the figure of Jesus Christ only in so far that it was through him that God had brought into being the new humanity, realized partially but really in the life of the Church. This he had done by raising the crucified from the dead, by bringing life through death. Therefore the essence of life in the Church was seen by Paul as, in some way, entering into or being conformed to the dying and rising of Jesus Christ, and so of passing through death to life – not simply in the sense of 'life after death', but in terms of present experience. 3. This basic experience Paul strives constantly to express in a confession of faith. Sometimes he is content simply to repeat and transmit the earliest forms of such a confession of faith, derived from the tradition (the 'kerygma'). At other times he emphasizes that form of it most relevant to gentile Christians ('Jesus is Lord'). But at other times again he is concerned to expand and interpret it in his own way, as for example in his teaching on the pre-existence of Christ, and on Christ's agency in creation and cosmic fulfilment. In this manner 'kerygma' is transposed into a different key, and so leads into theological reflection on a scale so great as to imply both a philosophy of history, and a metaphysics.

NOTES

1. See M. Dibelius, *Paul* (1953), chapter 4.
2. I Cor. 15.3.

6 John

The reader may perhaps be surprised that the chapter on the fourth gospel should be separated from those which deal with the first three. The NT seems to divide itself into two sections, the first half giving a historical account of Jesus, the second providing theological interpretation and drawing some practical conclusions. To put it differently, we are given first a record of *past* events, and then an account of the *present* faith of the Church. Well, we have already seen reason to question this neat division, because the synoptic gospels are found on inspection to contain a good deal of the Easter faith intermingled with the record of the pre-Easter events. Still it remains true that there *is* a past tense in the faith of the Church, as well as a present and a future; and the synoptic gospels are particularly concerned with this past tense, and to a much higher degree than is Paul and the other NT writers. Now because the fourth gospel ostensibly tells the story of Jesus just like the other gospels, it might appear that it belongs with them in being concerned primarily with the recording of past events. But it becomes apparent that in this gospel, as in Paul, the past, though vitally important, is overshadowed by a concern with the present and the future. All interest in recording the earthly career of Jesus has been absorbed into an account of the present experience of him as indwelling the believing community through the Spirit. The gospel tells us not so much what Jesus *had been*, but rather what he *had become* to the eyes of faith, and therefore what he was believed most fundamentally to *be*, *sub specie æternitatis*. If there is some justification for dividing the NT authors into the historians and the theologians, then John belongs more to the latter class than the former.

This overshadowing of the past by the present goes far to explain the differences between the synoptic and Johannine portraits of Christ, which we must now mention.[1] First, there is the enormous difference in the way in which Jesus is presented as disclosing himself. In the synoptics, the messianic claims of Jesus are made with the greatest possible reserve and indirectness; even the disciples are slow to grasp the truth, and when they do are sworn to secrecy. The fourth evangelist ignores this element of reserve and secrecy, and instead presents us with a picture of Jesus who at the very beginning of his ministry is hailed by various disciples as Messiah, Son of God, and King of Israel. His miracles are performed in order to 'manifest his glory', and his teaching in public revolves around the theme of his own person and destiny. Where the synoptic writers present Jesus as the one who proclaims the Kingdom, and himself only indirectly, the fourth evangelist presents him as one who proclaims himself consistently and constantly. All the way through this gospel the honour and majesty which believers had come to attribute to Jesus by virtue of the Easter faith is projected back upon the account of his earthly career, and all the honorific titles are placed upon his own lips.

Secondly, the rich synoptic picture of Jesus as a man who 'went about doing good and healing all manner of sickness among the people' has virtually disappeared, to be replaced by seven carefully selected episodes called 'signs'. Possibly these are derived from a special source used and adapted by the author. Moreover, these miraculous deeds are performed, not in response to faith (as in the synoptics), but in order to awaken faith, or to manifest Christ's glory. The episode of the turning of the water into wine is a 'sign' of the supersession of the insipid water of Judaism by the intoxicating wine of the gospel. The feeding of the multitude is a 'sign' of the power of the Son of Man to fulfil all the spiritual needs of men, to be himself the living bread from heaven, which bread is in fact his flesh which he will give for the life of the world. The raising of Lazarus is a 'sign' of Christ as being not only the giver of life, but himself in his own person 'the Resurrection and the Life', and it is also made clear in the sign that he gives life to others only at the cost of laying down his own. Each 'sign' has in fact a double reference. It first expresses outwardly the inner significance of the Lord's person. It also serves to interpret in advance the real meaning of a future event, namely the Passion, in which alone the full glory of Christ is to be revealed. In the perspective of this gospel the Passion, interpreted through the Resurrection, is the supreme, final and definitive 'sign' of God's glory in Christ, to which the earlier 'signs' are related as rehearsals to the drama, or as gesture to reality. Some of the Johannine 'signs' are the occasion of a discourse in which the theological significance is made explicit; in other cases the explanation is implicit in the narrative. But in every case the 'sign' is interwoven into the fabric of the gospel as a whole. This is one of the reasons why the 'signs' are so unlike the variegated and episodic miracle stories in the synoptic gospels.

Thirdly, the teaching of Jesus in this gospel is transposed into quite another key. Gone are the short, pithy, occasional sayings and aphorisms. In their place we find a number of carefully composed speeches, theological and hieratic in tone. Gone are the realistic encounters of Jesus with various groups and individuals. In their place we are given a number of stylized conversations, which are not really conversations at all, but rather studied and artificial dialogues, carefully mounted, oblique and suggestive rather than natural and spontaneous. Gone are the richly varied parables, to be replaced by a few great allegories (e.g. the Good Shepherd, the True Vine), totally different in style and purpose, and again self-consciously theological. Gone is the teaching on the Kingdom and the call to repentance and decision in relation to it. Instead, we have a number of carefully interwoven themes, all having to do with the relations of the Son with the Father, and the divinely ordered process whereby the Son returns to the Father, from whom he came, by means of his passion, which is, paradoxically, also his glorification. Gone is the teaching on judgment and salvation to come, to be replaced by a statement of the ultimate and ever-present tension between Life and Death, Light and Darkness – a tension which comes to focus in the encounter of the Incarnate with his enemies. Gone is the hope of a future Parousia of the Son of Man upon the clouds of heaven, to be replaced by the theme of Christ's present coming again to indwell his Church in and through the Spirit.

The episodic character of the synoptic record is thus replaced by a theological unity. The synoptic gospels present a series of detached sayings and incidents, each of which can to some degree be understood on its own. The fourth gospel is all of a piece. No section of it can be understood without reference to other themes in other parts of the book. Mysterious words and phrases like 'the hour' and the 'lifting up of the Son of Man' are announced in one place, taken up and developed in another, and finally resolved in the telling of the Passion story. The thought moves, as it were, spirally; everywhere there is the same allusiveness. Themes are stated, dropped, developed, restated, and integrated into one another, as in the unfolding of a symphony. Here we have a theological treatise in the form of a historical narrative; or else, a historical narrative which is told in such a way as to transform it into a theological treatise. Sir Edwyn Hoskyns puts it more vividly thus: 'The fourth gospel records not primarily what the crowd of eyewitnesses saw and heard of the Jesus of history, but what the disciples saw of the glory of the Word of God.'

Of course, it is possible that John had at his disposal a historical source (or sources) other than the synoptic tradition, which supplied him with some of the distinctive features of his gospel. The scholars are divided on the question of whether John is dependent on the synoptic gospels, or whether he is using and developing a source (or sources) quite independent of the synoptic tradition, and possibly in some respects historically superior. But whatever may have been the sources on which he drew, the author has so taken them into his thoughts and prayers and meditations, that they have become distinctively his own, and so come to comprise a transmutation both of the form and the content of the teaching of Jesus. The interest of the synoptic writers in what we have called the past tense of Christian faith was strong enough to make them preserve the form in which Jesus spoke his message, together with many characteristic features in the way he conducted his ministry. In John, however, the form no less than the content of Jesus' message and ministry have been absorbed into the single texture of a gospel which was written, not in order to give an accurate record of past events, but rather (in the words of the author) 'in order that you may believe that Jesus is the Christ, the Son of God, and that believing you may have life in his name' (John 20.31).

If, then, the history in this gospel is so wholly integrated into the theology, we want to know what was the background of the author's thought, what the dominating influences in his Christian experience, and what the audience for which he wrote. Unfortunately, there are no agreed and certain answers to these questions. Some scholars are impressed by the evidence for an early Palestinian origin for the sources used by the author. They point to the accuracy of the topographical notes, especially of the city and environs of Jerusalem. They emphasize the OT background to the symbolism, and draw attention to parallels with Rabbinic Judaism. Some claim to see a close conformity with some of the ideas to be found in the recently discovered literature of the Qumran sectaries from the Dead Sea, and think that this kind of sectarian Judaism has influenced the Johannine tradition at some point, possibly by way of the sect which revered John the Baptist. Those who take this view naturally tend to interpret all the great Johannine ideas by reference to a Jewish background. They freely admit that many of the expressions have a very Hellenistic ring about them, but think that these were used by the evangelist simply to 'ring bells' in the minds of some of his Hellenistically-minded readers, he himself being little influenced by them. He is thought to be like a modern preacher who might use words like 'evolution' or 'relativity' in order to capture the attention of his scientifically-minded congregation, without himself having much idea of what they meant, and without intending to pursue the line of thought.

Other scholars are equally impressed by the remarkable parallels between the language of the gospel and that of the higher thought of the Romano-Hellenistic civilization of the day. This 'higher paganism' was an amalgam of Greek philosophical notions (derived from Plato and the Stoics), oriental mysticism, Judaism, and a type of dualistic, speculative religion known compendiously as 'gnosticism'. These various ingredients later crystallized out into a kind of 'instant-mix' religious system described in a body of teaching known as the 'Hermetic Literature', and C. H. Dodd has drawn attention to remarkable verbal parallels between the gospel and this literature. Other scholars, like Bultmann, believe that there existed at this time a fully-blown myth of a heavenly redeemer, of a gnostic type, which had already entered into Christian thought, and that it was John's intention to restate the kerygma in these terms, while at the same time radically transforming them, and indeed, 'baptizing them into Christ', by attaching them to the historical figure of Jesus. Well, all this is a debate among the scholars, and there are no assured conclusions. The matter is further complicated by the fact that Jewish and Hellenistic elements had already combined in much of the first-century Judaism, both orthodox and sectarian. However, we shall not go very far wrong if we take the view that it was the intention of the evangelist to mediate the unchanging gospel to a changing world, and that meant to some degree Hellenizing it. W. D. Davies puts the matter in a nutshell when he says that the gospel has a *Palestinian root* and an *Hellenistic spread*.[2]

Therefore we may expect to find a double significance in all the great themes of the gospel, such as Light, Life, Glory, Judgment, the lifting up of the Son of Man. Both Jew and Greek would interpret these by reference to their own ways of thought. This double reference is seen at its clearest in the Prologue, where we read of the Word (Greek: *Logos*) who was in the beginning with God, and was God, and by whom all things were made. This expression, the Logos, would have carried a great wealth of meaning for both Jewish and Hellenistic readers. For the Jew, the Word or Logos of God was essentially God's self-communication to man, both in promise and demand. It was by his Word that God had created the heavens and the earth (see the Genesis narrative), and also had communicated his will to the prophets. In later Jewish thought this notion was combined with that of the divine Wisdom, i.e. the sum total of God's will and plan for creation, sometimes hypostatized as a pre-existent Being mediating between God and man. Still later this Word-Wisdom came to be identified with the written Law (Hebrew: Torah) given by God to Moses, and expanded and interpreted in the scribal tradition. The basic thought was of divine self-communication, culminating and consummated in the written Law. To the Hellenistic reader, the expression Logos would have had rather different connotations. To him the Logos was essentially the divine *reason*. The basic idea was one of order rather than of self-communication. Whether this eternal reality was conceived of in a pantheistic fashion, as in Stoicism, or as utterly transcendent, as in Platonism, in either case the basic notion was that of rationality and order, giving meaning to the totality of things.

So when the author begins his discourse on the eternal Logos, both Jew and Greek would have known what he was talking about. But when he goes on to state that the Word was *made flesh*, neither would have known at first what to make of such strange language. However, as the narrative proceeds, and the penny begins to drop, both would have been confronted with an immediate challenge to their respective preconceptions. For it now becomes clear that, according to the claims of this gospel, the self-communication of God, and indeed the very Thought or Mind of God,

c

has been finally and definitively embodied in the life of a particular human individual in all the concreteness of his personal existence in history. This called in question the Jewish presupposition that both eternal life and judgment had to be awaited in the future 'on the last day'. By the teaching on the Word made flesh, both are brought into the sphere of present experience, and indissolubly connected with the earthly career of Jesus.[3] It also called in question the Jewish dogma that the Law was the final word of God to man. The teaching on the Word made flesh clearly implied that there was a superior self-communication, in Jesus, superseding that given in the Jewish Law. But the Greek reader would find his presuppositions similarly called in question, and just as radically. For the teaching on the Word made flesh clearly implied that true and full knowledge of the unchanging Reality, of the eternal Thought or Mind, could *not* be achieved by any amount of intellectual effort or philosophical speculation, or mystical experience – but only by personal relationship with a particular figure in history, and that figure a singularly obscure and unimpressive one by normal standards. In other words, the criterion for understanding the eternal Logos is declared to be the personal activity of this man Jesus, an activity which reached its fulfilment in that perfect love (*agape*) whereby he laid down his life for his friends, and with which he infused his believers through mutual indwelling. Truth is not a thing to be attained by speculation or abstract knowledge, but only by the living of a new quality of life, whose embodiment is found in the personal activity of one man, within all the particularity and relativity of his historical existence.

So, then, the 'flesh' of Jesus, the concreteness of his existence in history, is central to the thought of the fourth gospel, and it is this which turns upside down and inside out all the familiar ideas, both Jewish and Greek, in which the author seeks to express his message. The glory of the eternal is seen in the transfiguration of a truly human life through a supreme act of self-giving in love. Jesus, then, is more than one person among many. Though a particular self, he is at the same time the true self of every man, and of the whole human race, standing in a unique relation with God, a relation which others can share only by dwelling in him. That is why in this gospel the earthly life of Jesus is presented, not as a concealing of the divine glory (as in Mark and Paul), but as a supreme revealing of it. The reason why John omits the story of the Transfiguration is probably because for him the *entire* incarnate life of Christ, and not just an isolated incident in it, is itself the manifestation of the glory of God.

But at this point it is vital not to get things wrong. It is most certainly *not* John's purpose to suggest that the outward and observable events of themselves reveal the glory of the Incarnate, as by some kind of compelling demonstration. If he had believed this, he would surely have been more careful about recording them exactly. The last thing he wishes us to understand is that neutral or hostile observers, like Pilate or the crowd, saw anything whatever of the glory of Christ, even if they did observe the 'flesh' of Jesus, i.e. saw his form and heard his words. It is simply because observable events are not themselves the revelation that the evangelist can be so free in the way he reports them. Indeed, he wishes to stress the importance of the observable, and the particular. Words like 'flesh', 'blood', 'Son of Man' – together with deliberately shocking expressions like 'Except you eat [literally 'munch' or 'bite to pieces'] the flesh of the Son of Man, and drink his blood, you have no life in you' – show an insistence on the full human reality of Jesus. But equally insistent is the idea that apart from the 'Spirit', i.e. the inward, God-given illumination, the 'flesh', i.e. the observable events, is of no avail. Exactly the same point is made by the play which the author makes on the twin expressions 'seeing' and 'believing'. For him 'seeing' is most certainly *not* 'believing'. There is a kind of 'seeing' which can exist without believing. Most of Jesus' contemporaries 'saw' him in this sense only. But when vision is accompanied by faith, then and only then does it lead to vision in a deeper sense; so that to see Jesus is also to behold his glory, glory as of the only Son from the Father.[4] This perspective is shown at its most compelling in what is the supreme paradox of the gospel, namely that the moment of Jesus' most complete humiliation is itself the fullest possible revelation of his glory. This accounts for the very remarkable dramatic irony with which the Passion story is told. To outward observation Jesus is condemned, humiliated, defeated. In reality it is the others who are condemned, and Jesus is shown as judge, king and victor – but only to the eyes of those who not only see, but also believe.

So it is only through the illumination of the Spirit that it is possible to see in the 'flesh' of Jesus the full glory of God. But more than once the startling assertion is made that the Spirit, described as the Counsellor (Greek: Paraclete) can only be given *after* the Son of Man is glorified (by way of the Cross), and *after* he has returned to the Father. It is the function of the Spirit to pierce the veil of flesh and reveal the glory there displayed. But this glory is nothing other than the glory of God's eternal and boundless love. Therefore it is only when he gives his life in total surrender that Jesus can reveal *this* glory in all its perfection. Only when the glory of the divine love (*agape*) has been definitively displayed in the 'lifting up' of the Son of Man, and only when this same divine *agape* has become known in the community of those who dwell in Christ and he in them, can the Spirit begin his interpretative work. The full glory of Jesus as the Word made flesh, though revealed all through his life, can be fully understood only the other side of Good Friday and Easter. This is hinted at early on in the words which comment on Jesus' mysterious words about raising up the temple of his body 'When therefore he was raised from the dead, his disciples remembered that he had said this' (2.22). It is made explicit in those passages from the Farewell Discourses where Jesus speaks of the Spirit, the Counsellor, who, after he is glorified, will interpret all that he has said and done, and will lead the disciples into all truth (John 14.26 f.).

Now perhaps we are in a better position to understand why the very great freedom with which the evangelist handles the tradition about the words and deeds of Jesus is in no way discordant with his theological position, and his purpose in writing. We can also see why he has mixed up the tenses, and projected upon the earthly Jesus words which the exalted Lord *now* speaks through the Spirit within the believing community.[5] We may perhaps go further and say that this procedure was not only consonant with, but actually necessitated by, his theological outlook. Only after the Son of Man had been glorified through his death, can the Spirit be given; only when the Spirit is given, can the true glory be fully known and understood. Therefore the best way in which the evangelist can be faithful to the truest and deepest significance of the words and deeds of Jesus in the flesh is radically to reinterpret them. This is precisely what he does both in the light of his present experience of the risen Lord in the life of the Church, and also in relation to the thought and outlook of his contemporaries.

One final point needs to be made. Although in this gospel Jesus is presented as, *par excellence*, the Revealer, yet it is also clear that what he reveals is nothing other than himself – himself as the mirror of the divine *agape*, and the embodiment of human response to it. Therefore in the very act of revealing this love, he brings into being a new community, with the new commandment to love one another, and a new power and possibility to fulfil this commandment, through their union with him. 'I am the vine, you are the branches.' To know the truth, and to have eternal life, is to be in personal communion with him who *is* the truth and *is* the life. So Christ prays 'even as thou, Father, art in me . . . that they may become perfectly one' (17.21–23). And when on Easter Day the risen Lord breathes on the disciples and says, 'Receive the Holy Spirit' (the Johannine equivalent of the Pentecost story in Acts), the language makes plain that what is envisaged is nothing less than a new creation, the bringing into being of a new human community, reconciled and reconciling, which is essentially inclusive of all humanity.

For Christ is not only the source of unity in the Church, but also the saviour of the world.

So in this gospel also we have the same interweaving of community, event, and message which underlies the NT as a whole. The characteristic feature of the Johannine gospel is the closeness of texture in which these three elements are interwoven, closer than in any other NT book. The characteristic feature of the Johannine interpretation of the message is the breadth of its scope, seeking as it does to relate the community-event to what is ultimately true of the whole of reality. It is universal in its spread, and metaphysical in its form.

NOTES

1. These differences, together with other considerations, are generally thought to preclude the possibility of apostolic authorship for the gospel as it stands.

2. *Invitation to the New Testament* (1967), p. 381.

3. See, for example, John 3.19 and 11.24–25.

4. See, for example, John 4.48, 20.6–10 and 20.29.

5. Most notably in the so-called 'high-priestly prayer' of ch. 17. Note the mixture of tenses there.

7 Unity and Diversity

It is a matter for regret that modern critical study of the NT has become associated in the minds of many with the purely negative connotations of the word 'criticism', rather than with the idea of constructive evaluation and interpretation. For critical scholarship has conferred the enormous benefit of enabling us to view the NT as the transcript of a living and developing tradition, and as the record of a community life. It has accustomed us to think, for example, of Mark, Acts, Paul and John as reflecting successive stages in the developing life and thought of the early Christian communities, and no longer to think of these writings 'in the flat', as components of a uniform and static system. By inviting us to look at the NT writings in this dynamic way, it has released us from the necessity to cling to a static and literalist interpretation less and less credible and relevant in relation to our own situation and ways of thought. In this way criticism has rendered a positive service in the propagation of the gospel. But it has also forced us to take very seriously the diversity of the NT writings, and so think out afresh the question of their basic unity. It is impossible in a book of this brevity to include specific comment on each book, but the reader is referred to the appendix and bibliography.

Unfortunately, this question of diversity and unity in the NT is inseparable from the presuppositions we hold about the nature of religious truth. Basically there are two approaches which, following Dr F. C. Grant, I will label the 'jig-saw puzzle' and the 'dominoes' approach. According to the first, theological truth consists in a number of self-contained propositions, fitting together like the pieces of a jig-saw puzzle into a neat and final pattern. Thus there comes a moment when the pattern is complete. Some would tend to identify this moment with the closing of the canon of scripture, others with the promulgation of the creeds, others with the production of some classical statement of theological truth such as the *Summa* of Thomas Aquinas or the *Institutes* of Calvin. Once this is completed, nothing need be added or subtracted – unless it be the discovery now and then of a piece that had got lost under the carpet, but had really belonged to the puzzle all the time, like the bit about the Immaculate Conception, or Double Predestination. The jig-saw puzzle conception is thus propositional in form, neat and tidy, appealing to the conservative outlook.

According to the other conception, the quest for theological truth is more like playing a game of dominoes. In this game the block first laid down asks, as it were, a question – a two-dot question, let us say. It is answered by a two-dot piece to match it. But the putting down of the second piece raises a further question, a five-dot question, perhaps, this time. So the game continues. Each added piece, while answering one question, sets a new problem, and initiates a new quest. God is good. How do we know? Because he sent his Son into the world to save us. But how could he, being good, allow his Son to die on the cross? Because in this way he proposed to overcome evil. But how could people be expected to understand this? Because it was foretold in the scriptures when correctly interpreted. How was it, then, that the people of Israel failed to understand their own scriptures, and rejected their own Messiah? Because God had hardened their hearts. But was this not very unfair? . . . and so on. Now this process is no more haphazard than that involved in the doing of the jig-saw. The central block is all-controlling, each piece demanding some particular other piece to match it; there are definite rules to the game, not any old answer to any old question. But unlike the jig-saw puzzle, you never know quite what is coming next, for it all depends on what piece your partner is going to put down next – and, of course, in *this* game of dominoes your partner may well be yourself in a different mood, or a changed set of circumstances. Moreover, the pattern is never completed. The game could go on for ever, for there is a limitless supply of pieces. Certainly the same old questions keep coming up, the same old two-dot or six-dot questions, but each time in a different setting. Basically they are the same questions, but asked with such very different slants, and in such very different circumstances, that the answers are always wearing a new look.

Those who hold this conception of the quest for theological truth claim that it is demanded by the very nature of the Christian faith, and that for two reasons. In the first place Christianity is all about a transcendent God who can be spoken of only in analogies and symbols, and it is well known that such things as analogies and symbols are in their very nature resistent to systematization, untidy and inconclusive. Secondly, Christianity is centred, not upon a proposition, but upon an event, interpreted as an act of the living God through the experience of a community, and producing a new way of life. When eternal truth is thus experienced as embodied in the stuff of human existence, then it is inevitable that the verbal expression of it will be as untidy and fluctuating as life itself must be, with lots of tiresome loose ends, everything open-ended always on the move. But for our purposes the reason for preferring the dominoes to the jig-saw model is that the nature of the NT itself seems to demand it. For here we are presented with an obvious unity, combined with an equally obvious variety. The NT revolves around one centre only, namely the event of Jesus Christ. But the theology in which this event is interpreted does not comprise a uniform pattern, like a completed jig-saw puzzle, but develops like a game of dominoes, striking out in this direction and that, by a process of question and answer.

Moreover, the use of the traditio-historical method forbids us to understand primitive Christian theology as developing methodically, and in a straight line, from the teaching of Jesus, through the early kerygma, to Paul and thence to John. Rather, it is shown as moving out simultaneously in a number of different directions, and organizing itself into what might be called 'areas' of thought – areas partly geographical, but more significantly cultural. The moment that Christians began to reflect upon their experience of Christ (as they did so reflect from the very start), they clothed it in those particular images and conceptions which were already live in their thought, and in terms of those particular needs, questionings and concerns which already exercised their minds and agonized their hearts. The fact that these varied from group to group, and from culture to culture, goes far to explain why early Christian theology took on such a kaleidoscopic variety of shapes and forms.

Let us take a few examples, first in the realm of Christology. If you were a Jew of Jerusalem, you would have been accustomed to thinking of God's final purpose in terms of the inauguration of a restored people of Israel through the agency of his anointed Servant, who would reign, like a greater David, in peace and righteousness. If you had then come to believe that this divine purpose was fulfilled through Jesus, you would naturally speak of him as God's righteous servant anointed to preach good tidings to the poor, thus clothing your new-found faith in the old and familiar forms. At the same time, you would be faced with the difficulty of fitting into this pattern the extraordinary and scandalous fact of Jesus' ignominious death at the instigation of God's own people. So you would go on to say that his death was 'according to the scriptures', i.e. foreordained in the counsels of God, and that God had in fact exalted this same Jesus by the resurrection, and so appointed him as Christ, or messianic king. This is the type of Christology (later called adoptionist, because it associated the Lordship of Jesus with his 'adoption' as Lord and Christ by virtue of the resurrection) which in varying forms is found embedded in some strands of the synoptic tradition, in the early parts of Acts and in the 'kerygmatic' passages of Paul's epistles.

But now suppose that you belonged to another 'area' of Jewish thought, and culture (in Galilee, perhaps), and had been brought up to think of God's final purpose in terms of the appearing on the clouds of heaven of a supernatural figure, called the Son of Man, who would destroy all evil and rule in God's name over a totally reconstructed heaven and earth. If then you came to see in Jesus the fulfilment of your hopes, you would naturally think of him as the one who would shortly come again in glory as the Son of Man triumphant, and who had already appeared 'incognito' in earthly form. This is the type of early Christology which we meet with in other strands of the synoptic tradition. In the completed gospels these two Christologies (with many variations) appear side by side, unreconciled but taken up into yet a different notion of Jesus as one who, in his earthly life, was already both Christ and Son of Man – though in a hidden fashion, his true nature being revealed only to the faithful with eyes to see and ears to hear.

Suppose now that, like Paul, you were a somewhat later convert, with no personal links with the earthly Jesus, who had been led to reflect upon the question: if Jesus in some sense *became* Lord and Christ by virtue of the resurrection, must he not have been so pre-ordained from all eternity? Suppose also that you felt quite at home with late Judaistic notions of the divine 'Wisdom' as a pre-existent Being through whom God created all things. Well, then, the stage is set for the great drama of the pre-existent Son, who, while being 'in the form of God' emptied himself to take the form of a slave, was obedient even to the death of the Cross, and was then highly exalted to the divine glory which was his by right, being given the name which is above every other name. Here we have yet another type of Christology, called 'kenotic', which sees the earthly career of Jesus as the total self-emptying of a divine glory, which belonged to him before and was restored to him again.

But then the question was bound to arise, how was it possible that the earthly career of Jesus should bear no trace of the divine glory which was eternally his? So there arose a third type of Christology which might be called 'incarnational', and which thought of the earthly career of Jesus as revealing and reflecting, rather than concealing, the divine glory which belonged to him by virtue of his perfect and eternal union with the Father. This type of Christology is seen in an incipient form in the synoptic gospels, but we have to wait until the fourth gospel before it becomes fully explicit. That it does become explicit here is due in large measure to the fact that in this 'area' of thought it found in the current speculation about the Logos, or universal rational principle, a ready vehicle for its expression. So there is not one standard Christology in the NT, but many types. Often earlier and later forms are found side by side in the same book. Sometimes early types survive subsequent developments and appear in quite late productions, as in Acts and I Peter.

We meet a similar diversity in the way in which the saving work of Christ upon the Cross is expressed. Sometimes this is conceived in terms of *victory*. In the synoptic gospels Jesus is presented as the one who wins a great victory over the demonic powers, under Satan their captain, who hold men and women in the bondage of evil and disease. In Paul and elsewhere he is the strong Son of God who, by his death, triumphs over the elemental cosmic spirits of the universe, who dominate world history. Exactly the same idea is expressed in I Peter, under the totally different imagery of Christ's descent into Hades, and in yet another way in Heb. 2.14. But elsewhere the work of Christ on the Cross is described in terms not of victory but of *expiation*, whereby the guilt of sin is removed. This idea is fully worked out in the Epistle to the Hebrews after the pattern of Jewish sacrificial worship. It appears in Paul, Hebrews and other books side by side with the victory motif, and without any attempt at synthesis. Then again in the fourth gospel, in addition to both these notions, we have the predominant thought of Christ as the divine Revealer, who by manifesting the true light dispels the darkness of error and disbelief, and so bestows salvation.

It is the same with eschatology. The first Christians were quite convinced that the saving work of Christ was final, but this conviction was bound up with the belief that soon the world would end, and Christ would return to reign for ever over a reconstituted heaven and earth, so inaugurating the 'new age' of apocalyptic expectation. But the world did not end, and he did not so appear. The result was that one of the most positive concerns of NT theology was to give adequate expression to this belief in the finality of Christ's saving work, but in the absence of any such demonstration of it. The various authors tread different paths. The least creative (the authors of II Peter, Jude and Revelation) simply put the expected event a bit further into the future, and try to keep people's spirits up by elaborating on the wonders of the cosmic firework display when it eventually happens. Luke substitutes for the apocalyptic hope the notion of the continuing significance of secular history, as the sphere in which the gospel is to be preached, and the Church catholic spread, under the direction of the exalted Christ. For Paul the two ages overlap, so that here and now a man may enjoy the 'first instalment' of the Spirit (viz. of the new age), though he looks for full realization hereafter at Christ's glorious appearing. In John, the belief in a 'second coming' of Christ has virtually disappeared, to be replaced by the thought of the present possibility of eternal life (or its obverse side of judgment) through the mutual indwelling of Christ and believers, in and through the Spirit.

All this variety in theological expression is matched by an equal variety in matters of church administration and political attitude. The type of church ministry reflected in Paul's letters is clearly different from that to be found in Acts, and different again from that in the Pastoral Epistles. It seems likely that there were two forms of eucharistic worship current in the early Church, each with different emphases. The conciliatory attitude towards the Roman government represented in Acts and in Paul's letters is in striking contrast with the bitter hostility towards the state which we meet in the pages of Revelation. So one could go on. Permeating it all is the sea-change effected by the transition from a Jewish to a Hellenistic environment. Thus the Johannine portrait of the incarnate Logos would have meant very little to the Palestinian Jew who hoped for the coming of the Son of Man upon the clouds of heaven, simply because the questions he asked of life were so different in form from those asked by the readers of the fourth gospel. Yet both he and they shared the same basic experience of new life in the Spirit, and the same burning conviction that God's final purposes had been achieved through the raising of Jesus from the dead. The dialectical process continually produced new interpretations, threw up new images, demanded new formulations. After the last book of the NT had been written, the process still continued – and continues still.

What is it then that makes the NT a unity? What is the *constant factor*? It can be summed up of course in the two words 'Jesus Christ'; but that summary needs clarification. Many of the usual answers are easily seen to be inadequate. It will not do to say that the constant factor is the NT itself, in its monolithic unity, and because of the inerrancy of its every statement. Apart from the other formidable difficulties in the way, such a view necessitates denying the evident variety of the NT witness, blurring the sharp edges of the books, distorting or obscuring the distinctive notes in the various strands, in the interests of a harmonization which is itself inevitably subjective and preconceived. Nor will it quite do to claim that the constant factor, as is often asserted, consists in the 'historical facts', understood as the mighty acts of God. For it has already been shown that the 'facts' as recorded are already ablaze with the faith of the Church, already inseparable from the very varied interpretations and images in which they are presented. Moreover, such a view is in danger of causing us to neglect vast expanses of NT material, especially in the epistles, not directly related to those allegedly observable facts. It is even more unsatisfactory to look for the constant factor in some synthetic formula, harmonizing all the NT ideas, and alleged to be the basic creed or kerygma of the Church in NT times. It is an impossible task. What is more, no possible permutation or combination of NT ideas could possibly do justice to the *freshness* of the emergent faith. There was surely something both novel and unique about the impact of the Christ event, and the experience which was bound up with it, which could not be contained in, or accounted for, by any combination or collection of the existing ideas, images, analogies or myths which were used to communicate and explain it. Notice, for example, how quickly the 'Son of Man' Christology, at first so prominent, just disappeared from the scene altogether, or was transmuted beyond recognition.

One other attempt to discover the constant factor remains to be considered, and that is the attempt to ground all the rich variety of NT thought in the teaching and self-understanding of Jesus himself. It is sometimes argued that the really creative theologian of the NT was Jesus of Nazareth, and that all the distinctive ideas of the NT may be traced back, more or less directly, to the way in which Jesus understood and interpreted his mission and destiny by reference to certain leading OT conceptions and images, which he combined in unique fashion and quite self-consciously related to himself. This view, namely that the teaching of Jesus was the supremely creative factor in NT theology, has been characteristic of British theology in recent years. But in the eyes of many it is based on a number of highly disputable assumptions, e.g. that Jesus possessed a developed, indeed highly sophisticated, 'messianic consciousness'; or that he made a deliberate and creative synthesis of such OT conceptions as the Son of Man in Daniel 7, and the Suffering Servant in Isaiah 53. The fact is that the records themselves do not supply anything like sufficient evidence on which to base such theories. Many, therefore, will prefer to hold the view that, although the things that Jesus said and did and suffered were certainly the controlling subject of NT theology, yet the creative use and reinterpretation of OT ideas and titles and categories used to express his significance were more likely to have been the work of others, reflecting mainly their own present experience of Christ, crucified and risen.

Well, then, if the constant factor is not to be found in the words of the NT itself, nor in any selection or harmonization of its various ideas, nor in the historical facts themselves, nor in the teaching and self-understanding of Jesus, it seems to follow that we must look for it in the actual experience which preceded and controlled all attempts to express and communicate it in words, or propositions or images. So we come back full circle to the conclusion of the argument in chapter 2. The unity underlying all the varied doctrine of Christ's person and work contained in the NT is an existential, not a propositional unity. Underlying all the varied and sometimes irreconcilable ideas and images in which the doctrine of Christ is expressed in the NT, it is possible to find in every part a self-understanding, a perspective on life, an encounter with God, which is indeed constant, homogeneous, and instantly identifiable. For want of a better term, we may call this constant element an 'experience'. But it must be said at once that this experience is: (a) communal and shared, not individualistic; (b) concerned with the totality of human living, not a matter of intermittent emotional states or 'religious experiences', though these may be involved also; (c) not static, but developing, the experience of being caught up in a movement, rather than held captive in an unchanging situation and (d) controlled throughout by the continuing impact of the Christ event which both originated it and continued to dominate it. The experience was in fact the impact which Jesus made upon his followers; and its perpetuation in the life of the Church, which grew up around it, may be said to be the very heart and centre of the Christian revelation. It is therefore the primary authority, to which all the varied conceptions and formulations used to express it are strictly secondary, and therefore capable of reform and revision.

Among modern theologians the one who has followed out this line of thought most consistently is the American scholar, John Knox.[1] He is quite clear in his mind that the saving act of God, which is the constant theme of the NT, is nothing other than the coming into being of the Christian community, in and through the things that Jesus did and suffered, as these things made their impact upon, and were appropriated by, the community. He speaks of the *miracle* on which the life of the Church is grounded. This miracle consists in the fact that, when Jesus is 'remembered' within the community, then he is experienced or 'known still' as living presence, so as to become the source of that distinctive quality of human existence and togetherness summed up in the word 'Spirit'. This inseparability of 'Spirit' and 'memory' whereby Jesus truly lives the other side of death in the midst of his own, is said to be the ultimate and irreducible mystery of the Christian faith. That is why Knox can say that the question about Jesus Christ can be thought of as a question about an *event* and a *community*, just as appropriately as a question about a person. When the question is asked in this form, then the implications for the problem of the unity underlying the variety of the NT are very clear, and can be seen in the following quotation:

It follows from this that the christological question does not need to be construed as a question about the person; it can just as appropriately be thought of as a question about the event or the community. And it is when we ask the question in one of the latter forms that the large and significant agreement in belief, not only among early Christians but among all Christians, is most likely to emerge. Let us suppose, for example, that we were accustomed to ask the question primarily about the event; that when we asked 'What think ye of Christ?' we meant not 'Who is he?' or 'Whose son is he?' (Matt. 22.42), but 'What has occurred?' 'How are we to understand this thing that has happened among us?' If this were the question, would not the answer have been something like this: 'In Christ, God has visited and redeemed us. The same God who made a covenant with Abraham has made a new covenant, calling into being a new people. He who made known his ways to Moses, his acts to the children of Israel, has acted now in the fullness of time to deliver mankind from all its enemies, from the guilt and power of sin and the fear and doom of death. This deliverance, although it can be fully consummated only in the age to come, God has brought about in our history and has made available in the new community of the Spirit to all who will receive it in penitence and faith.' Would not this have been the unanimous early-Christian answer if the question had been asked in this form, and would it not have been the answer in every part of the church in all the ages since?

Or suppose the christological question has been primarily a question about the community: 'What is the reality in which these persons who knew Jesus and now remember him participate, and which constitutes the essential principle of the community's existence?' Would not the answer have been rather similar? Something like: 'That reality is God's own presence and love – that is, his Spirit. Through the remembered event God has acted to bring into being this community, into which these persons have been called; in this community the One they remember is known as a living Presence, and in it are found the forgiveness, the healing, the security, the hope, they need. All of this is found there because God himself is present and active there and has chosen to bestow it there. It is the community of his Spirit.' And would not this answer have been unanimously given, through all the centuries, as the other?[2]

If the views of Knox strike some readers as too extreme and unbalanced, still it remains true that this line of approach seems to be gaining ground amongst modern scholars, and certainly opens up fresh avenues of exploration. Similar ideas are expressed in a more moderate form by Dr W. D. Davies, and we may note this passage especially:

The assumption behind the NT is that at a particular time, in a particular life, God was decisively at work; its concern throughout is to witness to these events. By this is meant not that it merely pointed to a person, Jesus of Nazareth; this alone would not have availed. Rather, it witnessed to him by appropriating his life and living in him so that his life was its life. The NT is concerned with events as they are appropriated and become alive in the lives of Christians:

Tho' Christ in Bethlehem a thousand times was born
Unless He was born in thee, thy soul's forlorn.

The gospel points to events which happened in the past, but are made present in the response of faith and life. It is these events *in this sense, that give unity to the NT.*[3]

Finally, and lest there be misunderstanding, this is not to say that the message by which the event and the community experience is expressed is unnecessary. Christian *doctrine* is always necessary, because it is the outcome of the community's reflecting upon the experience which brought it into being and sustains it, and also its attempt to communicate this same experience. It is also necessary in that the experience, however subjective in its appropriation, is of such a kind as to carry with it a genuine *truth-claim*, viz. a claim (though not a demonstration) that the experience points to a reality which is prior to and independent of it, and is indeed descriptive in some fashion of 'what is the case' about the universe. But the point remains that none of the propositions, doctrines or images, either alone or in combination, can be appealed to as the bed-rock and unifying factor in NT faith. Rather, all these variegated images and ideas must be allowed to co-exist, each illuminating and fertilizing the other, but without being confused or given absolute significance. An analogy from music might help. A movement in a symphony contains a number of themes or subjects, often contrasting, yet somehow comprising a unity. Yet this unity is not obtained either by playing only one theme and leaving out the others, nor by playing them all at the same time! Rather, each subject is announced on its own, then the subjects are related and developed in such a way that they react upon one another, then finally they are repeated but often subtly transfigured as a result of their interplay in the intervening development section. So, if we are looking for a doctrine of Christ which is really true to the rich variety of the NT witness, we shall look for one which, in the words of Dr F. C. Grant, 'will account for the range and variety of eschatological, metaphysical, and even moral ideas and attitudes, expressed not only in plain prose or description or exhortation, but also in hymn, prayer and liturgy, and likewise in personal devotion'.[4]

Appended Note on Pseudonymity

It is surprising how few of the NT books are put out under the name of the author. Most are anonymous, including all four gospels. But others appear to have been written under a name different from that of the real author, i.e. under what we would call a pseudonym. These include, almost certainly, the Pastoral Epistles (under the name of Paul), the Epistles attributed to Peter, James and Jude, together with many writings outside the canon of the NT. They *may* include Colossians and Ephesians, written under the name of Paul. It is natural, but none the less naïve, to call this process forgery. It might be forgery if practised today, with our conventions and ethics of literary production. But in the ancient world, both Jewish and Hellenistic, it would not necessarily have been so. In those days pseudonymity might be practised simply as a literary convention, accepted by both writer and reader, without any intention to deceive anybody. In other cases the author might attribute his work to his teacher, as an act of homage or humility, or because he wanted to set down, not his own thoughts, but those which he believed to be his master's. Or else, the device might be used to gain for the book a wider reading public than otherwise it might have had – not necessarily a dishonest thing to do, if the motive was not self-regarding, and in the light of existing literary conventions. Again, in the case of Christian writings, we have to remember that, in the early days of the Church, there was a strong belief that, when a Christian 'prophet' spoke under inspiration at assemblies for worship, his words were not his own but those of the Holy Spirit, and therefore in effect the words of the living Christ, directly or through his apostles. Such a belief, while still effective, might well spill over into written as well as oral utterances, and so account for the attribution of such writings to the Lord himself by way of his apostles. Again the motive was neither self-regarding nor deliberately deceitful, so that the charge of forgery is hardly in order.

Now if the revelation of God in Christ is thought of as being conveyed through the inerrant words of scripture, this element of pseudonymity is a real embarrassment. But the opposite is the case if, following the argument of this book, the revelation is located in the intensely varied experience of the Christian community under the impact of the Christ event in all its fullness. For in this case, the larger the number of witnesses we can find for this varied and creative impact (whether in the shape of individual authors, or community tradition, or both), the richer and fuller will be the revelation. Thus the Pastoral Epistles give us an insight into the way faith in Christ impinged upon the mind of a man other than, and different from Paul himself – and in a set of circumstances other than, and different from those of the apostle in earlier days. And that is pure gain. It is the same in the case of Peter. We know all that we need to know about Peter – the warmly human saint, the first witness to the resurrection, the chief of the apostles, the rock on which the Church of Christ was built – without any need to have recourse to the epistles which bear his name. If, however, we are allowed to see in I Peter not the work of the apostle but rather the production of a Church leader under the first official persecution (that under Trajan, c. AD 112), and if also we may detect in this letter a baptismal sermon (as many scholars think we can), then we learn a lot about how Christian faith related itself, both to official persecution, and also to the experience of sacramental worship in which it came to be expressed. And that too is pure gain.

To sum up: the NT provides us with a picture not of Jesus-in-himself but of Christ-in-the-midst-of-his-own, in relation to a great variety of individual and corporate needs, problems, and opportunities – spiritual, personal and intellectual. Such a view helps Christians today in their present task of relating the unchanging gospel to a very rapidly changing world. Therefore the greater the number of 'witnesses' to be found in the NT the better. The discovery of pseudonymous writings in the NT, in so far as it adds to this number, is gain and not loss.

NOTES

1. See John Knox, *The Church and the Reality of Christ* (1962).

2. John Knox, *The Early Church and the Coming Great Church* (1957), pp. 66–67.

3. W. D. Davies, *Invitation to the New Testament* (1967), p. 49. (My italics.)

4. F. C. Grant, *An Introduction to New Testament Thought* (1950), p. 62.

8 History

It has been argued in these pages that the NT is best understood as the transcript of the living tradition of a community,
originating in and controlled by an event (the things concerning Jesus), and expressing itself in a message (which
takes on a variety of forms). Moreover, these three elements
are inseparable, the recording of the event being strongly
coloured by the community experience, and the message
taking its shape from the interaction of the community and
the event. Now this immediately brings to focus the question
which the reader of these pages may have found himself
frequently asking, but which has not yet been properly
grasped. It is the question, what can we know with any
certainty about the event as it actually happened? What can
we know with reasonable certainty about what Jesus
actually said and did, on grounds of historical evidence?
There is also the related question: how important is it for
faith that such certain knowledge should exist?

Three preliminary comments need to be made.

1. The gospel records tell us at first hand what Jesus
had come to mean to the faith of the early Church, and thus
only indirectly what Jesus actually said and did in the
historical setting of his life and ministry. As we shall see,
what we can thus learn indirectly is considerable. But it is
vital to realize that we are not at liberty to take the records
as a direct eye-witness account without further question.

2. We are similarly forbidden to take the evidence simply
at its face value in a more general way, because such a
procedure is inconsistent with proper historical method.

This method demands that we do *not* take the evidence simply at face value, but rather that we sift it, put questions to it, apply certain tests to it. It is often said that one of the most vital characteristics of Christianity, which gives it superiority over other religions, is that it has its roots in real historical events. If so, we must draw the inevitable conclusion that the evidence for these events must be submitted to all the rigorous tests which are rightly applied to all other historical facts. In this sense at least, Benjamin Jowett was certainly right when he stated that the Bible must be treated just like any other book. Not to do so would show that we did not take its *historical* basis really seriously. One cannot in this matter have one's cake and eat it.

3. Conversely, and in order to maintain balance, it must be stated that the fact that the evangelists were governed by theological motives in the way they select, order and interpret the material about Jesus, does not in the least preclude the possibility, or even the probability, that they are *also* conveying historical reminiscences.

With these preliminary points made, we may now consider the first of our two questions. Is it *possible* to go behind the gospel records to discover what can be known with reasonable certainty, and by the use of strictly historical evidence, what Jesus actually said and did and was? An enormous literature exists on this subject, and it would be foolish to claim that the answer is settled. Nevertheless, certain guide lines seem to be emerging. On the negative side it seems to be clear that: (a) it is not possible to know anything very much about the order of events in the life of Jesus (beyond the barest outline) and therefore *no biography* can be reconstructed. The nature of the evidence does not provide the necessary material. (b) Nor does the evidence enable us to know much for certain about the *self-consciousness* of Jesus. We cannot tell by what process he came to a consciousness of his mission, nor precisely how he conceived it, or in what categories he expressed it. We do not know, for example, whether he made any explicit messianic claim. Still less do we know anything about his inner life and personality traits, how he prayed, what he looked like, whether he was genial or reserved, cheerful or sad, fiery or calm. But on the positive side it appears that (*a*) we can know quite a lot about the *teaching* of Jesus, and of his *self-understanding*, i.e. how he understood his own existence in relation to God's nature and purposes (though we do not know the process whereby this understanding was reached for that would lie in the realm of self-consciousness). Most scholars would also maintain that the impression of unparalleled intimacy with God his Father on the part of Jesus which the records convey has all the marks of authenticity.

It will be noticed that what modern scholars claim can be known about the Jesus of history is a good deal more modest than what older generations of scholars believed. The reason for this change of emphasis is that improved historical method has exposed the subjectivity and unscientific nature of much of the nineteenth-century 'Quest of the historical Jesus',[1] with the plethora of mutually exclusive 'Lives of Jesus' which it produced. For a time it came to be concluded that *no* knowledge of the historical Jesus (beyond the barest facts) was either possible or theologically desirable. But more recently a 'New Quest of the historical Jesus' has been pursued, by form-critical scholars themselves, more modest because more scientific. These scholars now have at their disposal a formidable workshop of sharply precise instruments by whose use they can dissect the gospel material into three main blocks: (*a*) that in which the actual words and deeds of Jesus do not lie far beneath the surface of the records, and can fairly accurately be separated out from the modifications they may have undergone in the tradition; (*b*) that in which fact and interpretation are too closely interwoven to be clearly distinguished, but where historical reminiscence still plays some part: and (*c*) that in which the developing faith, reflection and meditations of the Church have produced words of the Lord, and sometimes events, which in no sense belong to the course of his life on earth, but which in one way or another communicate what he had come to mean in the lives of believers.

It is not possible to describe within the short course of this volume the precise nature of these tools which have been perfected, nor the criteria which are used.[2] The important thing to note is that under the first head (what can be discovered about the teaching and characteristic actions of the historical Jesus) a quite substantial body of information is available. Even Bultmann, in spite of the scepticism in these matters which he professes, was able to write a book about Jesus, using only this source, whose length ran to over two hundred pages.[3] It is also worth noting that the tiny handful of students of the NT who still cling to the total scepticism of the 'Christ-myth' school (i.e. that Jesus never even existed, or if he did, that nothing can be known of him) are those who do *not* use the form-critical method; if they did, the absurdity of their position would be exposed.

Having given a provisional answer to the question whether it is *possible* to go behind the 'kerygma' and the gospel record to discover what can be known about the historical Jesus, we now have to ask whether it is theologically *desirable* or necessary to do so. Again there is an enormous literature, and the debate continues. There is no space to consider those important and intricate questions about the very nature of history, and historical study, with which this problem is intimately related. Leaving aside, however, these wider questions, there seems to be one important and indeed obvious sense in which historical knowledge about Jesus is desirable, perhaps necessary for faith. It is this. It is admitted that the gospel record presents us with a portrait of Jesus rather than an exact photographic representation, and that it portrays Jesus as interpreted through the Easter faith. But surely both faith and common sense demand that there should be some kind of real *continuity* between the portrait and the interpretation on the one hand, and the events as they occurred and are historically verifiable on the other. Granted that it is the interpreted Christ, the Christ of the Easter faith, who is the true object of faith; yet it would, to say the least, be odd to the point of absurdity if this Christ simply bore no relation at all to the Jesus of history, if the portrait bore no resemblance at all to the sitter. At this point the New Quest can help a good deal, because it presents us with a body of information about Jesus which, by the criteria mentioned above, may be said to be established, with greater and lesser degrees of certainty, as authentic and historical reminiscence.

Now this authentic material (the edges, of course, are very blurred) has been summarized and paraphrased so succinctly and lucidly by Professor D. E. Nineham in a recent television broadcast that I could do no better than quote his words in full:

Take the interpreted picture of Jesus presented in the gospels, and look for any passages which do not square with it – which have slipped through the interpretative net, so to say. For example, according to the church's interpretation, Jesus claimed to be Son of Man, and yet you come across a passage like this:

For whoever is ashamed of me and of my words in this adulterous and sinful generation, of him will the Son of man also be ashamed, when he comes in the glory of his Father with the holy angels *Mark 8.38*,

in which, at any rate on the most obvious interpretation, Jesus seems to *distinguish* himself from the Son of Man. The early church will hardly have invented such passages, for they seem to contradict its general picture of Jesus, so they are presumably original and provide a starting-point for a historical reconstruction. Clearly there is no room for dogmatism here, but this is the *sort* of line along which a good deal of recent scholarship has been working; and the upshot so far appears to be something like this. Although the historical Jesus probably differed in certain quite important respects from the picture conveyed by the finished gospels, he was in fact such that the gospel picture can be justly described as 'fair comment' – legitimate deduction from the genuine historical facts. If I may try to fill that out a bit, the first thing to notice is the 'authority' or the 'directness' of Jesus. In his teaching and activity he was not dependent on any support from outside himself. For example, he did not say, as the Rabbis tended to say, 'Things are thus and so because that's what the Old Testament means if properly interpreted'. Nor did he say: 'So and so's going to happen because if you add up the numbers in Daniel or Jeremiah that's how it works out.' He just boldly claimed: 'I tell you . . .'

And what did he tell them? That God's Kingdom was coming; they would soon be finding themselves face to face with God – inescapably involved in dealing with God, in a situation in which his will prevailed completely, and everything had been brought into conformity with it. Jesus probably envisaged this in terms of the end of the world and God's appearing with clouds descending and trumpets blowing, very much along the lines of contemporary thought; and he may have expected it very soon. But that is not really vital, because it was not the whole, or even the centre of Jesus' concern. He was not just concerned to point men to something God would do in the future – he believed God was *already* doing something in and through him. When he was able to cast out demons, for example, he interpreted that as God's power at work in him, starting the final overthrow of the forces of evil. And even more important, he believed that in his dealings with other human beings also God was at work. Jesus had certain attitudes and standards – he demanded honour, goodness, consecration, unselfishness and love – what he called 'perfection' – from everyone, and he would settle for nothing less; he would not abate his demands by so much as a jot or tittle. But yet, he welcomed people into his company and full friendship without their having come anywhere near meeting his demands. He freely gave his friendship to extortionists and prostitutes and all sorts of people who were nowhere near having attained the perfection he demanded. He called people to come and stand beside him, to adopt his relationship and attitude to others. They were to come without any pretence of having attained perfection; and yet without any fear of being rejected by Jesus. His principle seems to have been that his free acceptance of those who came into contact with him and the influence of his love on them would lead them to contrast their previous attitudes with his and would create this attitude in them. And all this he did in *God's name*. His attitude, he said, is God's attitude and if men have accepted his call and entered into relationship with him they are in that same relationship with God. Jesus' unconditional promise of love and acceptance was in fact God's promise made through him, so that in all he said and did he claimed to be confronting men directly and immediately with God. That was the meaning of his 'authority' and 'directness'. As one of the German scholars puts it: 'His attitude is not that of a prophet or a sage; it is that of a man who dares to act in God's place.

This means that as he saw it, people's relationship with God was essentially bound up with their relationship to him. To follow Jesus, to accept his call and forgiving friendship *is* to partake in God's kingdom, to be in the true relationship to God. Therefore Jesus believed that with his appearance the time of salvation had arrived; the time, that is, when people can enter into a decisive relationship with God. Jesus' aim was not so much to introduce a new concept of

God but to open for men a new relationship with God, a relationship which means the certainty of being accepted, and so freedom from anxiety, and thus sonship, liberty, simplicity and love.[4]

Now if there is any truth in this reconstruction – and there surely is a considerable degree of truth in it, even if some modifications are made necessary by further research – it establishes a real continuity between the words and deeds of Jesus and the faith of the Church through which these words and deeds are communicated in the gospels. To quote Professor Nineham once again:

When NT writers spoke of Jesus as a supernatural figure who had come down from heaven to live on earth, they were only drawing out, in the ways of speaking natural to them, the basic truth which Jesus himself had affirmed in his own way.

The facts on which the gospel interpretation is based are shown to be such as to make the interpretation, not indeed necessary, but plausible; not indeed demonstrable, but still 'fair comment'. Granted that the gospels present a series of imaginative portraits of Jesus, yet the techniques of modern scholarship can go far to establish a genuine resemblance between the portraits and him who was the subject of them.

To this extent the 'New Quest' performs a useful, perhaps necessary, function. However, it is important not to get it out of focus. For the real subject of the NT is not Jesus as a figure of the past, but Jesus as the Christ – that is to say, as the one through whom God acted for the world's salvation, so as to bring into being a new humanity, whose nucleus is the Church. It is, moreover, an essential element in the concrete experience of the Church that Jesus is not dead, but lives and can be known still, in and through the Spirit. But all this goes far beyond the scope of any purely historical judgment. The most that historical research can do is to hows that the facts as they happened are not incompatible with the supernatural interpretation with which faith invests them. Thus, historical research can establish that Jesus died, and perhaps that he died under a specific set of circumstances. It cannot possibly demonstrate that he died *for my sins*. This can be known only from within the community of faith. It is the kind of certainty which can only come from sharing in, and making one's own, the experience of those who were first exposed to the impact of the death of Jesus, and under that impact came to interpret it so. It can be neither established nor destroyed by historical research, even though such research might well cause me to take a different view about some of the facts underlying it (e.g. that some or all of the Seven Words from the Cross are not well attested). Again, historical research can certainly establish that the disciples believed Jesus to have risen from the dead. It *might* even establish that the tomb was empty. It could not possibly establish that God had raised Jesus from the dead and exalted him to the throne of the universe. Such knowledge can come only by belonging to that community whose present experience of the living Lord corresponds to that recorded of the same community under the initial impact of the events concerned. This, too, historical research can do nothing either to vindicate or overthrow, even though it might cause me to revise my estimate of the events underlying it (e.g. that the records of the Resurrection appearances contain legendary elements).

Knowledge of Jesus *as the Christ* is and must be mediated by the community of those who responded positively to the impact of Jesus upon them, and in responding interpreted it – sometimes by means of imagery and myth, sometimes by rewriting the history so as to bring out its deepest meaning. That is why the assertions of the NT which most directly communicate the saving knowledge of Christ are those which are most of all outside the scope of historical research, e.g. 'God so loved the world that he gave his only Son, that whoever believes in him should not perish but have eternal life'. That also is why the words of Jesus which most deeply communicate what he means for believers are those words which have arisen out of the Easter faith, and are the *least* likely to have been spoken by him in the days of his flesh, e.g. 'Come to me, all who labour and are heavy-laden and

I will give you rest', or, 'For where two or three are gathered in my name, there am I in the midst of them'. Under this head, too, we must place all the great words of the Johannine Christ, such as 'I am the bread of life', and 'I, when I am lifted up from the earth, will draw all men to myself'.

The last point raises the question of our attitude to those recorded words of Jesus which there is reason to believe not to have been utterances of the historical Jesus. Their purely historical value is by no means slight. Words which come to be attributed to any great figure in history tell us a great deal about him. The *kind* of words or opinions which are attributed to him throw light on the *kind* of person he was. If he were not this kind of person, these words would never have been confidently attributed to him. But words attributed to Jesus in the NT, though not actually spoken by him, can also possess a considerable *religious* value. For we surely need to question the assumption that there is something uniquely authoritative about the actual words of Jesus, in contrast to those placed upon his lips under the immediate impact of his death and resurrection. For to deny equal, or even superior value to the latter may betray an inadequate appreciation of the meaning of the Resurrection, and of the reality of the Spirit in the Church. Take, for example, the great farewell discourse of Jesus in John 13–17. These are not the words of Jesus, but the meditation of the evangelist placed upon his lips, a meditation arising very probably out of the evangelist's participation in the eucharist at which the Lord's death was continually brought to remembrance, and his living presence experienced. Surely we may not say that these words are in no sense the words of Christ? For here what was remembered of Jesus has been illumined and more fully explicated by the Spirit. In this sense, and as Dr W. D. Davies puts it, 'we may be more in touch in these chapters with Jesus himself than if we simply had his own words. The dormant meaning of his words has been awakened for us by the Spirit informing the great author of the Fourth Gospel.'[5] It would certainly seem to be the case that our knowledge of the authentic words of

Christ is not limited to what can be established as the words of Jesus in the flesh.

But what about those *stories* about Jesus in the gospel records whose literal truth we may feel bound in all honesty to question? Obvious examples are the story of the coin in the fish's mouth, or the resurrection of the saints in Jerusalem after the crucifixion of Jesus. But there are also the Christmas stories in Matthew and Luke, the 'nature miracles' such as the Stilling of the Storm, and above all the great dramatic episodes in John, such as the Changing of Water into Wine, and the Raising of Lazarus.[6] We may be convinced by the evidence that they could have happened just as recorded; but suppose we are not? Well, perhaps it is really only part of our modern materialistic way of looking at things which causes us to work on the unconscious assumption that truth can be conveyed only through the prosaic statement of brute fact, and not at all through poetry, legend, symbol and myth. Perhaps God's repertoire is more varied than we supposed. Perhaps he is able to reveal himself not only through the historical facts of Jesus' life, but also through causing certain stories to be told about Jesus, which bring out the deepest meaning of his person and destiny. After all, in secular history it is inevitable that every really great man should have 'tall stories' told about him, and it is often these stories which tell us as much about the man and his impact as do the straightforward accounts of his life. Not that I am suggesting for one moment that some of the gospel episodes are just 'tall stories', they are much more profound than that. But their power to communicate the impact of Jesus upon his disciples, both then and now, need not depend on their strict accuracy in every case. Such a realization enables us to be more relaxed in our approach to them, and enables us to be open and receptive to what the evangelists really mean us to understand by them; and this always has to do with the reader's present relationship to God's purposes in Christ. We shall be less open and receptive in this way, if we are constantly bothering our heads, as we read, with trying to sort out exactly what is fact, and what is interpretation. When Luke tells the story of the Saviour's birth, he is not interested primarily in recounting certain interesting or remarkable tales about past events. He is seeking to communicate, through stories about origins, what is most profoundly true about Jesus in God's eternal purpose, and about the salvation which Jesus has achieved, a salvation in which the reader is invited to share. If I listen to these stories, anxiously striving to convince myself of their historical accuracy, it is likely that I shall be unmoved by them, and my Christmas will be spoilt. But if, as I listen, I meditate upon the question, 'What kind of man is this of whom such ravishing tales are told so soon after his death?' and 'What am I being asked to believe about this man in relation to *myself*, my life and attitudes and relation to God, here and now?' then I am more likely to 'get the message' the writer intends, and my celebration of Christmas will be enriched.

Two things must be said, however, by way of reservation. 1. To question the historicity of *some* of the gospel episodes does not mean throwing doubt on *all* of them. We are not to lose our heads. As we have seen, historical research can establish the high probability of the salient facts. The stories may then be adjudged 'fair comment', even if in themselves not literally true. 2. It must not be supposed that those who tell these stories (if stories they be) were simply 'making them up', still less intending to deceive. Probably they arose quite gradually out of the corporate life and worship of the church, and consist in imaginative and interpretative embellishments of genuine reminiscences. When a Jewish rabbi wanted to draw a deeper meaning out of an OT episode, he would do so very often by embellishing the episode with imaginative and fictitious embroidery, i.e. by telling fresh stories around the subject. *We* would keep the historical episode and our own interpretative comment separate; they did not. It is important not to attribute to early Christian teachers and prophets the same canons of historical method and literary ethics which we practise today.

Now to return to the main question of this chapter: to what extent does a saving knowledge of Christ come through the 'kerygma' of the Church (with its literary expression in the completed gospels), and to what extent through establishing the events as they happened by means of the 'New Quest' of the historical Jesus? An analogy may help. Suppose that I am a master at an approved school, and I have heard about one of my predecessors, who has been dead some years, and who had the reputation of having exercised a wonderfully transforming influence over the boys in his charge. I want to learn about him, in order to get inspiration for my own task. Two courses are open to me. I can try to discover as much as I can 'objectively' about the man by carefully planned research, examining letters and documents and exam results, interviewing a number of impartial observers, and so on. In this task I may leave aside the evidence of the boys themselves (now grown up), because their evidence is likely to be 'biased'. By these means I may succeed in obtaining a remarkably accurate reconstruction of the facts relating to the man's career, but it will be comparatively lacking in inspiration; it will not help me much to be a better teacher. Or else, I can leave all this research aside, and go direct to the boys themselves, and find out from them what kind of impact and impression the master actually made on them. In this case I shall be meeting the man in and through the changed lives which resulted from his career. Well, the picture I get of him by this means will be a good deal less accurate than by the other. In certain respects it will not quite tally, certain traits will be exaggerated: some 'tall stories' may have intruded. But it inspires me, and I feel in this way much closer to the man than ever I did by means of the more strictly historical research. Moreover, I can test the reality of it by the extent it helps me to become a better teacher of my own boys. Now, if I have any sense, I will use *both* methods, because both are necessary, and they are not mutually exclusive. The first acts as a control to avoid credulity, and establishes the man's reputation upon a number of hard facts, enough to make it plausible, though not to demonstrate it conclusively. Thus it is purely supportive. The second method is the only really effective way of obtaining a 'saving' knowledge of the man, and it must consist in actually participating in the life and witness of those who first responded to him, and were changed by him. This analogy, like all analogies, is imprecise and must not be pressed – particularly as it hardly touches upon the supernatural, transcendent reference inseparable from any consideration of the gospel records. Still, it may help a little to place the 'New Quest of the historical Jesus' in its proper perspective.

NOTES

1. The title of the English translation of A. Schweitzer's monumental work *Von Reimarus zu Wrede*, first published in 1906.

2. See R. H. Fuller, *A Critical Introduction to the NT* (1966), pp. 94–103.

3. *Jesus* (1926); Eng. tr., *Jesus and the Word* (1935).

4. *The New Testament Gospels* (1965), pp. 34–37. See also articles by the same author in *The Church Quarterly Review*, Jan.–Mar. 1965, and in *The London Quarterly and Holborn Review*, Apr. 1967.

5. W. D. Davies *Invitation to the New Testament* (1967), p. 467.

6. The NT references for these episodes are: Matt. 17.24–27; Matt. 27.51–53; Matt. 1 and 2; Luke 1 and 2; Mark 4.35–41; John 2.1–11; John 11.

9 Present Interpretation

The need to interpret and make relevant the scriptures has always been a primary concern of Christian teachers and preachers. Every theological student knows that the third part of the sermon must be the 'application'. The problem is not new. Yet so acute is it today that a new technical term has been invented to describe it: hermeneutics. By this word is meant the principles which should govern any attempt to expound and apply the ancient text of the scripture. It greatly exercises the minds of theologians, especially in Germany, and is producing a considerable literature of its own. Why the fuss?

First, because the old idea that a text of scripture could be first expounded as a kind of divine oracle, or infallible proposition, and then 'applied' to a present problem in a mechanical and external kind of way is impossible for us. It is just not as simple as that. Because of our historical approach, and the different conception of divine revelation that goes with it, the question is bound to be split up into two tenses: What did it mean then?, and, What does it mean now? Try as we may, we cannot escape the difficult enterprise summed up in the oft-repeated and now famous words of Dr Leonard Hodgson, 'What must the truth have been, and be, if it appeared like this to men who thought and spoke like that?'[1]

Secondly, the enormous advances made by biblical historical scholarship in recent years – its attempt to deal descriptively with biblical ideas without smuggling into the description later doctrinal presuppositions or modernizing notions, its concern really to get under the skin of the biblical authors, to see through their eyes, and think their thoughts – these advances have served to bring into relief the great *distance* between their outlook and ours. Great NT scholars like Johannes Weiss and Albert Schweitzer, for all their one-sidedness, have forced us to recognize that the teaching of Jesus and of the first Christians was cast within the strange and bizarre setting of late Jewish apocalyptic, with its emphasis on the end of the world. Rudolf Bultmann has opened our eyes to the affinities between many NT ideas and the equally bizarre gnostic speculations current in the ancient world. Krister Stendahl puts the matter thus:

> Do these old documents have any meaning for us – except as sources for our knowledge of a small segment of first-century life and thought, or as a means for a nostalgic visit to the first era of Christian history? If they have a meaning in the present tense and sense, on what grounds do they have this meaning?[2]

Thirdly, this sense of distance has been further accentuated by the vast revolution in human thought produced by the Enlightenment and the rise of modern science. It certainly seems to be the case that, up to quite recent times, there was sufficient affinity between the thoughts and assumptions of the men of the NT period and those of Western European man for the ideas of the NT to be accepted and handled much as they stood. But ever since the enormous advances in scientific and historical knowledge begun in the mid-eighteenth century, the ideas and assumptions which modern man holds on almost every subject are poles apart from those held by the NT authors.

So we ask the question: if these ancient documents still have meaning today, on what grounds do they have it, and on what principles may it be discovered? We may first note three inadequate answers. In the first place, it will not do to say that simply by concentrating on the actual subject-matter of the NT (God, Jesus, grace, salvation, etc.) the bridge between the centuries will be overcome because divine revelation stands above history, and transcends it as by a miracle. This is the view of Karl Barth, and so one must be careful, for it is unwise for pygmies to snipe at giants. Still, it can be safely said that this element in Barthian theology no longer commands wide acceptance. It fails to do justice to Bultmann's point that the understanding of any word or document necessitates some congeniality between it and the person who hears or reads it. If a man in this century is to make anything of the NT texts, then they must 'chime in' at some point with the way he looks at things, and the questions he asks of life. And if these are, in many respects, different from those implied in the texts, then the problem of interpretation remains, and cannot be got rid of simply by appeal to a theological principle. But secondly, it will not do either to go along with an older generation of 'liberal' scholars, and simply try to reduce the NT material to certain general principles, considered to be of 'permanent value' or some such phrase. Such a procedure makes mincemeat of the texts, and is hopelessly subjective and unscientific. Thus Father Tyrrell, that great Roman Catholic modernist, once remarked that the portrait of Jesus obtained by such procedures was simply a Liberal Protestant face, seen at the bottom of a rather deep well. What is more, these scholars were just as convinced as their conservative opponents that the essence of NT faith could be adequately expressed in terms of certain basic propositions; they were simply concerned to substitute different ones (e.g. the universal fatherhood of God and the brotherhood of man, instead of salvation by the blood of Jesus, or the like). But we have seen reason to doubt whether the essential reality of the NT faith can be properly or definitively expressed in any set of verbal propositions, whether traditionalist or liberal.

A third and equally unsuccessful attempt to deal with the difficulty is by appeal to the Bible as a record of the 'mighty acts' of God within what is called 'salvation history', by which is meant a great cosmic drama, beginning with the creation of the world, centring in the saving work of Christ, and culminating in his coming again in glory at the end of the world. Historical events are substituted for propositions as the foundation principle of interpretation. As we shall see, there is an important truth in this approach, but, in the naïve way in which it is often expressed, it also will not do. For one thing it tends to limit the divine activity to a certain section of history, and to evacuate the rest of it of any meaning. But also, the idea of 'salvation history', if understood more or less literally as the working out of a divine time-table in human history, is only possible on the small-scale view of history characteristic of the ancient Semitic world. But what becomes of it when the time scale is extended by millions of years forward and backward? Must it not be said that, when Christ failed to appear in glory to roll up the scroll of earthly history soon after the resurrection, then this entire conceptual mould was, if not smashed to bits, at least badly damaged? The attempt to express the essence of Christian truth simply in untranslated terms of a view of history belonging to the ancient world looks like a piece of archaism. Granted that the early Christians expressed their experience of the finality of Christ, and of the urgency of the gospel message, in terms of a belief that the world would come to an end at any moment, yet is it not absurd to think that we ought to force ourselves to believe (against our better judgment) that the world *may* end tonight, in order that we may then have the satisfaction of a greater sense of urgency?

Then let us consider two other approaches to the problem which look more promising, and which reflect the two ways in which modern theology in general is progressing. The first we may call, for convenience, the personalist, and the second the historical. The personalist approach is that adopted by the great existentialist theologians of the Protestant churches, and it is also characteristic of one branch of progressive Catholic thought. Its NT inspiration is the fourth gospel, and Paul in some of his moods. It finds its most extreme expression in Bultmann's programme of demythologizing, and it will be most convenient to outline it in this form, since space forbids a fuller or more balanced treatment. For Bultmann, the real purpose of the NT affirmations, whatever their form, is neither to state a doctrine, nor to convey facts about the past, nor to present a philosophy of history. Though many of its statements are cast in this form, their real intention is to effect a change in man's understanding of himself in relation to his world. They challenge his old self-understanding, with its clinging to false securities of one kind or another, and thus open fresh possibilities of living. The 'events' of which the NT speaks are of little value simply as events, but only in so far as their recitation is potent to effect a change in a man's perspective and self-commitment in the here and now. History as such has no meaning, except in so far as it provides the occasion for a man to change his decisions and commitments.

Bultmann goes on to point out that the events of which the NT speaks are not bare facts, but are everywhere interpreted within the framework of a story about the universe, which he labels 'myth'. He uses this word, not in the popular sense of a kind of fairy story, but in the technical sense of a method of conveying existential truth, or more exactly as a means of challenging man's self-understanding. It speaks of the supernatural in terms of the natural, of the other-worldly in terms of the this-worldly. The mythology of the NT is not uniform, but its elements are familiar. The pre-existent Son of God descends from heaven, or else Christ is born of a Virgin; the Saviour on the Cross offers an expiatory sacrifice, or else wins a victory over the demonic powers; he is raised from the tomb, or ascends into heaven, or is exalted to the Father's right hand; he sends the Spirit, and will come again in glory on the clouds of heaven at the (imminent) end of the world. Not only is this the language of 'myth', says Bultmann, it also presupposes a cosmology, a world-view, which is utterly remote from our own. It presupposes a 'three-storied universe' of earth, heaven and hell; and regards the earth itself as the scene of constant interventions of supernatural agencies, both divine and demonic, so that man is never in control of his environment. Such a world-view is impossible for modern man, with his vastly improved knowledge of history and of the universe;

and Bultmann writes in a famous and provocative sentence: 'It is impossible to use electric light and the wireless and to avail ourselves of modern medical and surgical discoveries and at the same time to believe in the NT world of demons and spirits.'[3]

What are we to do? We may not, says Bultmann, 'select' the bits from the NT which we find congenial, nor may we *eliminate* the mythology. What we must do is to *interpret* it in such a way that it conveys the *real* challenge of the Cross, while freeing us from the *false* challenge to believe things which we find frankly incredible. This may be done by asserting the principle that the real purpose of the mythological statements is, not to provide an objective picture of things as they are (outside our own subjective awareness), but to be a mode whereby we may be won from a false to a true understanding of our own existence, and thus to be summoned to personal decision. To demythologize is to de-objectify the NT language about heaven and hell, angels and demons, supernatural events and personages. Thus no statements about God and the acts of God can have any meaning unless they are at the same time statements about ourselves, unless they affect our attitudes and decisions. The myths are to be interpreted *existentially*, i.e. in terms which challenge our present attitudes and call us to decision. When the NT speaks about the domination of Satan, or evil spirits, or 'principalities and powers', this tells us nothing about the nature of the universe. Rather, this language serves to awaken in us an awareness of our own state of enslavement, deriving from a false self-understanding and an 'inauthentic existence'. (The analysis and terminology here is drawn from existentialist philosophy, particularly that of Heidegger.) So long as a man believes that he must control his future and achieve his security by putting his trust in the visible, tangible and manageable realities – money, pleasure, power, ambition – he is a prisoner of his own self-imposed anxiety, he is in no way open to the future, and he is unable to love and be loved. Now when the NT goes on to speak of Christ as the one who has won a mighty victory over these hostile demonic powers (or alternatively has effected an expiation from the guilt of sin), again this has nothing to say about the world and its history. Rather it serves to open up the possibility of a new self-understanding, an 'authentic' existence. It makes possible that freedom which comes from faith, from being open to the future, from being prepared to accept as a gift the recognition we need, rather than anxiously to strive to wrest it from others, and from God, on the basis of our own achievements. So when the NT speaks of Jesus Christ as having descended from heaven, or as being Lord and Saviour, or born of a virgin – all these are different ways of expressing the basic truth that the passage from inauthentic to authentic existence is effected, not from within ourselves (here Bultmann parts company with the existentialist philosophers he has been following), but only from a liberating Word which comes from beyond, from God – and that this divine Word is spoken in the event of Jesus Christ as appropriated by faith. All the mythological statements (e.g. that the Father sent the Son, etc.) are ways of saying that the historical events surrounding Jesus of Nazareth have been so taken up out of the flux of time that, under God, they may become for every man the means whereby God's word of love and grace is spoken so as to liberate him for new possibilities of living. This is what is meant by speaking of the Christ event as *eschatological*. Indeed, in Christ God draws near to man in grace and mercy – not in Jesus as a figure of the past, but only in the way he is proclaimed, through the preaching, to the here and now of personal, ultimate decision. Thus the cross is not some kind of external transaction whereby a supernatural personage atones for our sin, nor an event of the past which expresses a general and timeless truth. It is rather a permanent reality, originating in a past event, but made present through the proclamation in the everyday life of the Christian, giving him present assurance of the liberating love of God towards him, and so offering him the possibility to be 'crucified with Christ' to his old inauthentic existence. The resurrection is not to be thought of as a miraculous event, somehow proving the divinity of Christ, but as a way of expressing the saving power of the cross. Thus to believe in the resurrection means so to commit oneself to the way of the cross as to find in it an altogether new possibility of living, victorious and fulfilling; and this precisely is what is meant by rising again with Christ.

So much for the personalist/existentialist approach. We turn now to consider the other principle of interpretation which we have called, rather inadequately, the historical. It is related to that second branch of modern theology which emphasizes the social and cosmic, rather than the purely personal structures of reality. This in its turn may be sub-divided into those theologies which see the gospel in terms of man's social and political life, and in his secular concerns, as in the writings of Harvey Cox, and in the thought of some modern Roman Catholic theologians, especially among the Dominicans; and secondly into those which attempt to place the Christian faith in the context of a cosmic scheme based on evolutionary process, as in the writings of Teilhard de Chardin, and the American exponents of 'Process Theology'. It tends to appeal for NT support to the writings of Luke–Acts, and various passages in Paul which convey either cosmic speculation (Rom. 8.18–25; Col. 1.15–20) or a philosophy of history (Rom. 9–11). The exponents of this type of interpretation claim that the basic categories of NT thought are those of time and history, rather than of essence or of existential truth. The basic notion is that of an ongoing history, and particularly of the ongoing religious life of Israel as the chosen people of God in the world. Putting the matter in rather an over-simplified way, it could be said that the grand theme of the Bible is God's purpose to serve the world and save the world through the presence in the world of a people chosen by himself, and entrusted with a divine promise and a divine commission. This people of God, however, has attained its self-understanding through certain events in its own history, which it has learned to interpret as the acts of God – the call of Abraham, the exodus from

Egypt, the return from Babylon, the death and resurrection of Christ. Yet these events are never thought of as 'bare facts' of the past, but are constantly interpreted (by means of saga, tradition, myth and ritual) so as to provide ever new possibilities in the present and future. Moreover the recitation of the past events is often so completely intertwined with the interpretation for the present and future, that one cannot be clearly distinguished from the other. Thus the common denominator in biblical understanding is the ongoing life of a people, a community, who cultivate the tradition of its history in the light of its corporate self-understanding in the present. This is just as true of the New Testament as of the Old; but in the New the consciousness of being chosen of God is intensified and universalized, and the event which is both remembered and constantly interpreted so as to control the present and affect the future is nothing other than the 'things concerning Jesus', centring upon his death and resurrection.

It follows that the hope of a future consummation of God's purposes in history is an essential element in biblical faith as interpreted in this way. But this hope does not receive its character from some preconceived blueprint of that consummation, or from any traditional form of expectation (e.g. the restoration of Israel's national glory, or the glorious coming of the Son of man in the near future). It receives its character from what the community has *already* experienced of the gracious purposes of God as mediated in its own history (the exodus, etc., for old Israel, the Christ event for the new). This means that the future hope can change its shape and form. It means also that the Church can survive and indeed be strengthened by the experience of immediate hopes deferred or disappointed e.g. the disappointment experienced by the first Christians when the Lord did not soon return in glory, or by twentieth-century Christians when the nineteenth-century missionary vision of a whole world converted to Christ failed to be realized. What is more, it means that the Church is open to fresh hopes unseen by former generations of Christians –

so that technological and medical advance, scientific progress, the enrichment of civilized existence, the unification of mankind, are by no means to be excluded from the terms of this hope simply because they formed no part of that hope in biblical times. Those who uphold this principle of interpretation are not to be confused with the exponents of a view of 'salvation history' which would seek to confine the saving activity of God to 'what happened in the Bible'. Rather such an approach recognizes that God is still the God who acts in history when he leads the Church into new and unexpected areas of human concern. It is not nostalgic, but open in its style. Many would go further and add that God's activity in Christ (and in the life of the Church) is not to be thought of as in any way exclusive, but quite the contrary. Schubert Ogden puts it thus:

> The NT sense of the claim 'only in Jesus Christ' is not that God is only to be found in Jesus and nowhere else, but that the only God who is to be found anywhere – *though he is to be found everywhere* – is the God who is made known in the word that Jesus speaks and is.[4]

In other words, God's act in Christ is the bringing to focus of that divine activity which is everywhere present. Thus the destiny of the Church, as God's people, is not to bring God to places and people from which or from whom he is altogether absent, but rather to be God's interpreter, bringing to light, witnessing to, co-operating with God's saving activity whenever and wherever it is to be detected.

But we must not stray too far from the basic theme of this section, which is simply to present a principle of biblical interpretation which appeals to history itself as the bridge which can cross the chasm of the centuries. It is in agreement with Bultmann's approach in so far as it insists that the ideas and myths of the biblical record must be interpreted in terms of our present self-understanding, but insists that, if we are to be true to the NT itself, we must recognize that this self-understanding is that of a community, and not merely of the individual; and that it includes within it a positive sense of the ongoing life and worship and mission of the Church in the world, God's world. It is not in direct opposition to the programme of demythologization, but again insists that there is an element of the corporate and of the historical which is resistant to thoroughgoing demythologization, at least in the terms in which Bultmann expounds it.

It is not the purpose of this chapter to make any choice between these two principles of interpretation, but simply to describe them. It is easy to detect the weak points in each. The personalist or demythologizing approach is vulnerable to the charge that, by reducing the gospel to the idea of present personal decision, it ignores the importance of the permanent, pervasive work of the Holy Spirit, operating at levels beneath the conscious mind, and working through the continuing life of the Christian community, particularly through regular participation in the sacraments. Its conception of self-understanding may be said to be too individualistic, too unrelated to the corporate life, fellowship and mission of the Church, too much separated from the roots of materiality and the historical process. It may also be charged with ignoring the possibility that some (not all) of the NT myths are in fact indispensable, because they have become irreplaceable, the actual bearers or carriers of the Church's life and power. Though we must be prepared, in Tillich's phrase, to 'break the myths' (i.e. to recognize them for what they are, and not as literal truth), yet this does not mean that they can be dispensed with, any more than poetry can retain its power simply by being turned into prose. On the other hand, the historical principle of interpretation is also open to objection. It may be said to do less than justice to the primacy of the personal in Christian faith, and to ignore the fact that the personal realm is for the most part highly individual, restricted in scope, having to do with everyday realities rather than with great historical or cosmic processes. This approach has a tendency to identify Christian truth too completely with particular philosophies of history or cosmological speculations, which are themselves relative and liable to be replaced by others. It may tend to forget that the historical categories and ideas of the

NT stand themselves in need of demythologizing. It is easy to detect the weak points. Still, it is very hard to deny the important and creative insights contained in both principles of interpretation. Evidently the two approaches, if regarded as closed systems, are mutually exclusive. But must they be taken as closed systems? May they not both contain true and complementary insights? Amongst some continental theologians the issues appear clear-cut, and the battle is on. In England and America there is less willingness to accept this as a straightforward either/or choice. But then it is perhaps the special genius of Anglo-Saxon theologians to be able to reconcile, or at least hold together, apparently contradictory viewpoints, without wanting to close the system, or run to extremes.

It will be obvious from this discussion that the problem of hermeneutics is closely bound up with that of the authority of the scriptures. If the scriptures are given supreme or sole authority in the understanding and communicating of Christian truth, then the question of how these ancient documents are to be made relevant to contemporary issues, and in the light of modern knowledge, is bound to be agonizingly acute. An exalted view of scriptural authority as the Word of God must result either in a naïve fundamentalism, or in the working out of a precise, not to say sophisticated, set of principles of interpretation. But if the scriptures are *not* set in isolation, if they are so to speak 'de-sacralized', and allowed to stand alongside other sources of Christian truth (tradition, reason, prayer and liturgy, secular insights and so on) then the problem loses some of its urgency and becomes more manageable. It then becomes possible to be much more relaxed in handling the scriptural texts, and not to feel tied to any one principle of interpretation. So this consideration of the problem of hermeneutics leads us into the subject of our final chapter, viz. the authority of the New Testament, and its status as 'sacred scripture'.

NOTES

1. The notion appears in various forms in the writings of Dr Hodgson, as in, for example, *For Faith and Freedom* (1968[2]), p. 88.

2. See his brilliant article 'Biblical Theology (Contemporary)' in the *Interpreter's Dictionary of the Bible*, to which I am indebted for some of the material in this chapter.

3. See H. W. Bartsch (ed.), *Kerygma and Myth* (1953), p. 5.

4. *Christ without Myth* (1961), p. 168.

10 Authority

One of the central problems, if not *the* central problem, for theology today (as indeed for philosophy, morals and politics) is that of authority. The old authorities are collapsing all around us. Yet we are aware that without some authority human life and thought disintegrate entirely. What seems to be clear is that the old authorities will continue to be effective only if they are brought out of their splendid isolation, freshly interpreted in relation to one another, and thus cut down to size. Something of the sort would appear to be true of the NT. The absolute and isolated authority once attributed to it is crumbling. We can no longer appeal to it in order to provide a set of propositions miraculously preserved from all possibility of error, and a set of ready-made answers to all questions. We can no longer appeal to it as giving an exact straightforward report of certain historical or scientific facts. It is difficult to regard it as, in isolation, uniquely inspired and uniquely inspiring, without denying the present and continuing power of the Spirit to lead into all truth, and thus denying much that is in the NT itself.

Our need is to develop an understanding of the NT which will allow it its proper authority as a controlling norm and point of reference for Christian faith and practice, without absolutizing it in such a way that it closes our mind to fresh truth and paralyses our ability to grapple with fresh problems and areas of human concern. It is at this point, as it seems to many of us, that the modern critical approach to the Bible can most help us. For this approach invites us to see the NT, not in isolation, but rather as wholly interrelated with the ongoing life of the Christian community and the Christian movement in human history – an ongoing life which both preceded the NT writings and continued after them, and indeed is still developing today. In this respect the NT has no authority which can be said to be independent, absolute, or unchangeable. On the other hand, this same approach allows us to attribute to the NT a genuine uniqueness, in so far as it comprises the only record we possess of the impact of the saving act of God in Christ at its initial point, and as such possesses an authority which is irreplaceable.

Let us take these two points in turn, and in reverse order. First the NT possesses an irreplaceable authority in that it provides us with the most direct access we possess, or are ever likely to possess, to that event, that primal 'disclosure situation' centring upon Jesus Christ, through which it is believed that God has spoken to us once for all in his Son. As such there is an element of finality about it. We have already spoken of this event in relation to the community in which it occurred, and which gave it its meaning. The event and the community, we have said, cannot be separated. Yet in one important sense the event has precedence over the community which grew up around it, and apart from which the community would not be what it came to be. Professor John Knox writes of the matter in these words:

To say that the event has this normative value is to say that the earliest period of the church's life has an importance which no subsequent period can have. The first age of the church reflects and embodies the event in its initial character and impact in a way no later age can hope to do. To be in touch with the most authentic life of the primitive church is to be in touch with the original event – the most direct touch we can have. It is correct to say that we can know Christ only through the church; at this point the Catholic idea is true. But when we say 'only through the church', we do not mean only through the contemporary church or even the church through the centuries. For it is given us to have contact directly with the primitive church, the church within whose experience the event occurred in a sense in which it cannot occur within ours, and whose experience has therefore a normative significance, unique in degree and kind. This direct contact with the primitive community is made possible through the Bible.

The authority for the Christian, then, is the authority of the event, for our knowledge of which in its initial impact we are dependent upon the experience of the primitive community which it called into being. But we are put in direct touch with this experience only in and through the documents which that community produced. Here we have the clue to the understanding of the paradoxical character of the Bible's relation to the community. On the one hand, it is less than the church because it grew out of the life of the church and has meaning only within the context which that life still provides, but on the other hand it is greater than the church because it brings us the only record we have of the event through which not only the community was brought into being but also its nature and reality must be constantly renewed. This is the ground of the Bible's authority.[1]

It is in this sense that the NT may be said to possess an authority which is unique, irreplaceable and final. But there is the corresponding truth that the NT, in so far as it reflects the Church's continuing and developing response to the event, and at one particular stage of its history, is wide open to further understanding and development as this same Church meets new demands, and is presented with fresh opportunities and challenges. So the passage just quoted has to be balanced by another passage by the same author, in which he writes:

The basis for these statements is the simple fact that the church is all we have – that is, all we have as Christians. It is true that we have the New Testament; but the New Testament is the creation of the community and brings us only the experience and thought of the community. To be sure, the New Testament has the unique value of giving us a kind of immediate access to the event as it originally occurred; but the event occurred only within the life of the primitive church and can be found only there. The New Testament gives us access to the event only because it makes us, in a real sense, participants in the experience of those to whom it was first occurring. As we read the New Testament, we become witnesses of the original event, not by getting 'back of' or 'beyond' the primitive community, but by getting more deeply into its life. For there is no access to the event except as it is remembered and embodied in the community.[2]

When Knox writes 'by getting more deeply into its life', it must be understood that this was a developing life, in

114

which neither theological understanding nor practical organization stood still. It was moving, and moving fast during the very period when the NT books were being written. Therefore the NT must be seen not as a book tightly sealed up at both ends, containing a body of timeless truths, but as the deposit of a living stream of tradition at a particular period of the Church's life. The word 'tradition' is here being used not in the sense of rigid forms and patterns, resistant to change, but rather in the sense of a living social process continually changing, continually in need of criticism, yet rooted in certain constant factors of common memory and values and perspectives. Understanding the word in this sense, let it be repeated that the NT is the deposit of a living stream of tradition at a particular period of the Church's life. The stream was already flowing before any of the books came to be written, so that the books themselves are part of the stream. Nor did the stream cease to flow when the last of the books were completed. It is impossible and misleading to draw a hard and fast line between the canonical and non-canonical books of the first two centuries. Moreover, some of the earliest liturgical texts at our disposal doubtless take us back to a stage in church tradition earlier than many of the NT writings.

And the stream still flows. The Christian movement in history continues. That process, so apparent in the NT, whereby the unchanging gospel took different forms as it encountered unaccustomed needs and challenges, is still with us today, and especially today. Therefore it is hard to attribute an authority to the NT which bears no relation to what might be called the 'contemporary mind' of the Church – so long as it is appreciated that this 'contemporary mind' is no more fixed and static and monolithic than the stream of tradition itself, for it *is* that tradition in process of further development. The NT itself is the record of a new upsurge of spiritual vitality which convinced the Church that God had acted to give a new direction to all human life, and had therefore opened up new possibilities and opportunities of human discovery and adventure. We may therefore agree with F. C. Grant when he writes 'with such a book in its hand the Church cannot fail to be adventurous – and to be prepared to see new things in our time, great and wonderful and unexpected, as the Spirit leads us where he will.'[3] That is why it is so tragic when the NT is interpreted in so wooden and authoritarian a fashion that it stifles rather than stimulates such fresh exploration into God's purposes for mankind.

After all, as we have already seen, plenty of new territory was being explored within the period of the NT itself. When the Church discovered, partly under the influence of Paul, that the gospel not only invited, but necessitated the breaking down of all barriers between Jew and Gentile, and when it then committed itself to the mission to the Gentiles, this was the exploration of new territory. When Hellenistic concepts were substituted for purely Jewish categories of thought, as in the writings of Paul, John and the author to the Hebrews, again fresh territory was being explored. The remarkable shift of emphasis in connection with the future hope of Christ's coming, so notable a feature in Luke–Acts and in John, likewise represents the exploration of fresh territory. So we have good reason to look to the NT to stimulate, rather than to inhibit, fresh explorations into truth in the present day. We have good reason also not to separate the NT from what we have called the contemporary mind of the Church, as it explores new avenues of truth and commitment, under two pressures. The first of these two pressures is the vastly extended knowledge of the universe brought to light by modern science, together with new understandings of the human condition revealed by modern psychological and sociological research, and the new and previously undreamed of possibilities opened up by technology. The second pressure is that of the Spirit in the Church, giving greater sensitivity to the Christian conscience, as a result of which some elements in scripture and tradition, previously dormant, are brought to life; and other elements, previously accepted without much question, are discarded or modified on grounds of being in fact sub-

Christian. In all these explorations which the very essence of the NT invites, we shall expect to find that the NT will continue to act as a stimulus, catalyst and control – but not in such a way as to inhibit the direct activity and guidance of the Spirit in the here and now. It may help to look at a few examples.

1. In earlier periods of the Church's history the doctrine of the everlasting torment of the wicked in hell, more or less literally understood, was normally taken as axiomatic, and indeed in the medieval period held a quite central place in Christian theology and practice. Today the doctrine has quite lost its hold, and few Christians of sensitivity and intelligence would want to countenance it. Now this remarkable shift in doctrinal emphasis did not come about as a result of Bible study, or on the grounds of the Bible's authority. The witness of the NT is notoriously ambiguous on the point, and a number of passages can be quoted in support of the doctrine. It came about through the present work of the Spirit (as faith would see it) making the Church more sensitive to the mind of Christ, in such a way as to liberate it from certain ideas which are now seen to be incompatible with that mind, even though these ideas should appear to be contained in holy scripture itself. Here we have an instance where the authority of the Spirit, working through the contemporary mind of the Church, serves to modify and qualify the authority of the NT – to qualify but not to abolish. For once the new insight is appreciated, then the NT can be read with fresh vision, so as to draw new inspiration from some passages previously neglected or obscured, such as the passages where the work of Christ is presented in terms of ultimate reconciliation (e.g. Rom. 9–11; Col. 1.15–20).

2. It took the Church nineteen centuries to tumble to the fact that the institution of slavery is utterly irreconcilable with the gospel, and the mind of Christ. Today nobody would ever deny it. Whence arose this discovery? Certainly not from reading the NT, for in these pages slavery is everywhere taken for granted, and never challenged as an institution.

The discovery arose out of the present work of the Spirit revealing directly to the Church aspects and implications of the mind of Christ hitherto concealed, even in the pages of scripture itself. Yet here again the discovery, once made, serves to give new depths and dimension to many of these NT passages which speak of Christ's reconciling work, breaking down all barriers between man and man, and reversing values.

3. We have recently witnessed the (painfully slow) formation of a common mind in the Church on such social issues as the emancipation of women, and the abolition of capital punishment. At this present time the Church is engaged in the painful process of coming to a common mind on such issues as contraception and population control, the laws concerning divorce and abortion, the morality of homosexual acts, etc. Very soon it will be faced with far-reaching and inescapable decisions about medical ethics, life and death, eugenics. Yet all these enquiries have to go on without direct reference to the NT. For in some instances (e.g. the place of women in society, the nature of homosexuality) the NT references can be positively misleading in that they reflect the social relativities and limited knowledge of their time. In other instances the NT has nothing direct to say, because at the time the issues were utterly unheard of. In all these matters, it would seem, the Church must learn to rely on the contemporary and direct guidance of the Spirit into the mind of Christ in relation to our present needs and problems. The authority of the NT must come in at a further remove as one of the ways, perhaps the most important way, in which that mind may be discovered in general terms.

4. One of the great new facts of our time is the rise of modern science, and the breath-taking new possibilities for human living and culture opened up by modern technology. It is quite impossible for Christian theology not to be deeply concerned about the way all this bears on Christian faith and practice. Many contemporary Christian thinkers are giving a very positive significance to technological

advance as being one of the means which God is offering to men to use (or tragically misuse) in realizing that fullness of human personalness which is his will for man, and whose full potentialities are already realized in Jesus Christ.[4] Again, such theological exploration cannot be carried on simply on the basis of the NT alone, for it belongs to a perspective wildly beyond the range of vision of the NT authors, and radically different from the way they expressed their hope. This exploration must be carried on in reliance upon the present guidance of the Spirit. Yet once it is embarked upon, then certain aspects of biblical teaching, certain mysterious hints and suggestions, suddenly come to life and begin to operate as pointers in the search (e.g. the conception of man made in the image of God in the Genesis narrative, and the teaching of the NT on the cosmic Christ, together with such particular passages as Rom. 8.18–25).

It would seem, then, that the authority of the NT is misconceived if it is not seen always as being in dialogue with that leading into truth which is the present and continuing work of the Spirit. The authority of the NT must never be viewed in isolation from all these other ways in which God wills to speak to his Church. These ways include the living tradition, the community experience of Christians, especially through liturgy and sacrament, the insights of prophets, scholars and theologians. But they also include the things which God is revealing about his world through the advance of secular skills and sciences, as these interact upon Christian insights and understanding. The distinctive and unique quality of the NT authority lies in the fact that, by bearing direct witness to God's saving act in Christ, it sets the direction for the search, points the way, and forms the one and indispensable point of departure.

The inevitable corollary which appears to follow from such a view of the matter is that it is necessary to distinguish between what is essential and non-essential in the NT witness to the mind of Christ, between what is of permanent relevance and what belongs to the relativities of a particular culture, between that which clarifies the truth of the gospel and that which tends to distort it. This raises the enormous question of what the criterion is to be, a question too large to tackle here. All that need be said here is that the difficulties inherent in a task are a poor excuse for evading it, especially when in any case it cannot be for long avoided. Indeed the NT may be regarded as the record of the way in which God enlightened the minds and hearts of certain men to see in certain events (the things concerning Jesus) the occasion of his full and final self-disclosure. But in so enlightening them there is no reason to think that he removed either their freedom or their common humanity. Consequently, these men were bound to express that which they had understood in terms of a particular culture and of particular forms of thought, which themselves belonged to a particular stage of human development and so lack finality or incorrigibility. Equally certainly, these men's understanding was bound to be in some ways affected by their own sins, ignorance and prejudices, so that what God was seeking to reveal was to that extent bound to be obscured. Even the recorded words of Jesus in the gospels bear the marks of such distortion on the part of his interpreters, as in the vitriolic character of our Lord's denunciations of the scribes and Pharisees in the Gospel of Matthew, and in the anti-Semitic flavour of some of the Johannine sayings. Must it not be said that one of the functions of the Spirit of truth is to enable Christians to distinguish between those ways in which the NT record truly communicates the mind of Christ, and those ways in which it partially or wholly obscures it? Has it not worked out like this in actual practice? The fact that the sifting process is often rough-and-ready, and largely unself-conscious, does not make it any the less real. Of course, such an idea is likely to scandalize those who are wedded to a strict application of the principle '*sola scriptura*' – no truth except in scripture. But then such a principle cannot be derived from scripture itself, and many would hold it to be incompatible with it. Nor will this way of thinking commend itself to those who hanker after a closed system of theological thought. But the NT itself hardly encourages us to think of

Christian faith in such a way. As Professor C. F. Evans has often remarked, none of the NT books seem to know how to end. They do not close up a system. Always there is a 'something more', which 'something more' belongs to God, and not to human contriving. Systems are useful, but never final. The Church may use them, but must never be dominated by them or enclosed within them.

In the first chapter the point was made that the habit of treating the NT as one volume of sacred scripture, as a 'holy book', has tended to obscure the meaning of the various parts of it. It might be helpful to end on the same note, and raise the question posed by the conception of sacred scripture, of a holy book, not in order to solve the issue but to stimulate further thought. There are some who want to cling to this conception very tightly indeed (even if it is admitted to be in need of reinterpretation) on the grounds that the possession of a sacred scripture is one of the divinely intended 'marks' of the Church. Only if the Bible is treasured and given supreme authority as the Word of God, they would say, can the Church be preserved from error, corruption and imperiousness. There must always be a process of reformation under the Word of God. They instance the numerous occasions on which the Church has been saved from corruption and perversion because of the sheer strength of this direct appeal to the scriptures – as for example in the brave struggle of the Confessing Church in Germany against the attempts of Rosenberg and his 'German Christians' to nazify Christianity. It is further argued that only on the basis of a sacred scripture, acknowledged by all, can there be any hope of ecumenical advance and ultimate unity. Certainly there must be development, but it is pointed out that this can take a wrong direction, and therefore there must be a constant 'exposure to the original', to use an expression of K. Stendahl. Nobody could possibly deny the cogency of these arguments.

Others, on the other hand, while not denying the important place of the scriptures in Christian faith and practice, would wish to ask whether the notion of 'sacred scripture' or of a 'holy book', understood as a self-contained and final court of appeal in all matters, belongs to the infancy rather than to the maturity of the Church. They would point to the ever-increasing distance which separates us from the world of the NT. To look but a relatively short distance into the future, one is bound to ask what it will be like for the Church of the thirtieth or fortieth century, if it has to look for its sole authority and supreme inspiration to documents belonging to a period of such remote antiquity. Even today, many find that the exclusive use of scriptural readings in public worship make that worship duller, more remote, and less relevant than it should be. Already less emphasis is being laid on the Bible in the religious instruction of the young. The problems facing the Church and the world are such that the ancient scriptures are becoming decreasingly useful in providing any direct or definitive answers.[5] What is more, it is difficult to deny that the appeal to a finally authoritative sacred scripture has in the past been used to support and justify any amount of devilry – religious persecution, hostility to scientific advance, witch-hunting, anti-Semitism, sexual repression, to mention but a few. So run the arguments, and again it is hard to deny their cogency.

This is an important debate, and is likely to increase in intensity. The only point which might usefully be made here is that the modern, critical approach to the NT books which sees them in the closest relation to the ongoing life of the Christian movement in history, is perhaps the one most likely, in the ultimate analysis, to re-establish them on a firmer footing, and thus guarantee their continuing relevance and validity. It is able to attribute to them this relevance and authority without necessitating the impossible corollary of absolutizing them in any way. When all is said and done, the books of the NT will continue to be irreplaceable as the only record we possess which gives primary access to the act of God in Christ which brought the Church into being, and apart from which the Church would not be what it has been, and still is. Moreover, these books, by virtue of their proximity to the source of the stream, contain such a depth and richness that their power to inspire and direct is inexhaustible. Even if the whole notion of 'sacred scripture' were to be wholly abandoned, the place of the NT in the Christian scheme of things would still be secure. The NT can stand on its own feet. It supplies a need which can be supplied in no other way. Does it require the support of any extraneous dogma of sacredness, infallibility or anything else? The question is worth asking.

The same God who is believed to have inspired the writing of the NT books may well be thought to be capable also of inspiring a new approach to those books which will ensure their continuing vitality as the record of God's word to man in Christ. It will be an approach which will assert their givenness and finality, without denying their openness. It will affirm their inexhaustibility as the Word of God, while gladly allowing that, for this very reason, ever new treasures may be found in them, as they make contact with fresh areas of human knowledge and concern. It will enable the Church to place the highest value on them, without making the mistake of over-valuing them, or isolating them from other sources of truth, or of putting them to uses for which they were not intended. It will enable the Church to continue to appeal to them as a norm, an indispensable point of departure, without at the same time creating out of them a strait-jacket to stifle and restrict all creative exploration into truth.

NOTES

1. *Criticism and Faith* (1953), pp. 62–63.

2. *The Early Church and the Coming Great Church* (1957), p. 49.

3. *An Introduction to New Testament Thought*, p. 42.

4. See, for example, David E. Jenkins *The Glory of Man* (1967), especially chapter 5.

5. It is interesting to note that in the storm of controversy aroused by the Pope's Encyclical 'Humanae Vitae' on contraception, the appeal to Scripture figures very little in the arguments used on either side of the debate.

Appendix

Note The information given here is based on the majority view of modern scholars. All of it is open to review in the light of further research, and none of it is to be regarded as conclusive.

St Matthew's Gospel Anonymous, author unknown, written perhaps at or near Antioch, c. AD 90.

St Mark's Gospel Anonymous, author unknown, but perhaps the John Mark mentioned in Acts and the Pauline letters, written between AD 65 and AD 75 at Rome or Antioch.

St Luke's Gospel Anonymous, author unknown but perhaps Luke, the companion of Paul, written c. AD 85, possibly at Caesarea.

St John's Gospel The original gospel (chapters 1–20) is anonymous. The appendix (chapter 21) has an appended note attributing the whole gospel to 'the disciple whom Jesus loved', usually identified with John the apostle. Most scholars deny apostolic authorship. Written between AD 90 and AD 100 from Ephesus or East Syria.

The Acts of the Apostles A sequel to St Luke's Gospel, the double volume often being referred to as Luke–Acts.

Romans Written by Paul, at Corinth, c. AD 56.

I and II Corinthians Written by Paul, consisting of several fragments of correspondence with the Corinthian Christians, written at various times between AD 53 and AD 56.

Galatians Written by Paul, between AD 49 and AD 56.

Ephesians Pseudonymous, attributed to Paul, written between AD 70 and AD 95.

Philippians Written by Paul, while in prison in Caesarea, Ephesus or Rome, between AD 54 and AD 62.

Colossians Probably written by Paul from Caesarea, Ephesus or Rome between AD 54 and AD 62.

I Thessalonians Written by Paul, from Athens or Corinth, c. AD 51.

II Thessalonians Pauline authorship disputed; if by Paul, written c. AD 51; if pseudonymous, c. AD 70.

The Pastoral Epistles (I and II Timothy, Titus) Pseudonymous, author unknown, written between AD 95 and AD 105.

Philemon Written by Paul while in prison at Rome, Caesarea or Ephesus, between AD 54 and AD 62.

Hebrews Anonymous, author unknown, written between AD 85 and AD 95.

James Pseudonymous, written towards the end of the first century.

I Peter Pseudonymous, written by an unknown author between AD 90 and AD 112.

II Peter Pseudonymous, incorporating most of Jude, written by an unknown author, between AD 100 and AD 125.

I, II, and III John Anonymous, author or authors unknown, but from the same provenance as St John's Gospel, written towards the end of the first century.

Jude Pseudonymous, written by an unknown author between AD 100 and AD 125.

Revelation Written by an author called John, otherwise unknown, on the island of Patmos, near Ephesus, c. AD 90–AD 95.

For Further Reading

DAVIES, W. D. *Invitation to the New Testament* London: Darton, Longman & Todd, 1967.

FULLER, R. H. *The New Testament in Current Study* London: SCM Press, 1963.

ROPES, James Hardy *The Synoptic Gospels* Harvard University Press, 1934; Oxford University Press, 1960.

KNOX, John *Criticism and Faith* London: Hodder & Stoughton, 1963.

Jesus, Lord and Christ New York: Harper, 1958.

The Death of Christ London: Collins, 1958: Reissued in Fontana Books, 1967.

BORNKAMM, Günther *Jesus of Nazareth* London: Hodder & Stoughton, 1960 (first published in Germany, 1956).

ZAHRNT, Heinz *The Historical Jesus* London: Collins 1963 (first published in Germany, 1960).

HUNTER, A. M. *The Gospel according to St Paul* London: SCM Press, 1966.

NOCK, Arthur Darby *St Paul* Oxford University Press (Home University Library), 1946.

HOWARD, W. F. *Christianity according to St John* London: Duckworth, 1943.

GRANT, Frederick C. *An Introduction to New Testament Thought* New York: Abingdon Press.

Index